D1643634

The Crowned Lions

By the same author

The Making of a King: the Early Years of James VI & I
James V, King of Scots
The Life and Times of Edward II
The Stewart Kingdom of Scotland, 1371–1603
The Kings and Queens of Scotland

The Crowned Lions

The Early Plantagenet Kings

Caroline Bingham

David & Charles

Newton Abbot London North Pomfret (Vt) Vancouver

British Library Cataloguing in Publication Data

Bingham, Caroline
The crowned lions.
1. Henry II, *King of England* 2. Richard I, *King of England* 3. John, *King of England*
4. Great Britain – History – Angevin period, 1154–1216
I. Title
942.03'092'2 DA205

ISBN 0 7153 7515 6

Library of Congress Catalog Card Number

Typeset by HBM Typesetting Limited
Standish Street Chorley Lancashire

Printed in Great Britain by
Redwood Burn Limited Trowbridge Wiltshire
for David & Charles (Publishers) Limited
Brunel House Newton Abbot Devon

Published in the United States of America
by David & Charles Inc
North Pomfret Vermont 05053 USA

Published in Canada
by Douglas David & Charles Limited
1875 Welch Street North Vancouver BC

Contents

Illustrations

'We came from the Devil, and to the Devil we will return.'

(a saying attributed to King Richard I, of his family)

THE ROYAL H

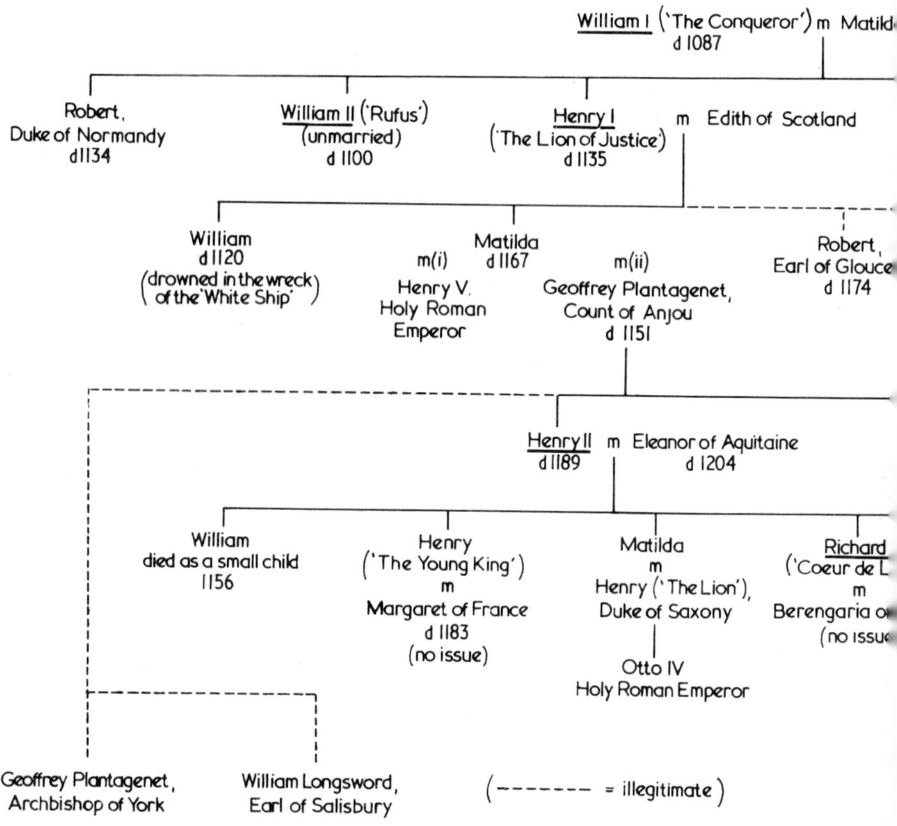

William I ('The Conqueror') m Matild
d 1087
Robert,
Duke of Normandy
d 1134
William II ('Rufus')
(unmarried)
d 1100
Henry I
('The Lion of Justice')
d 1135
m Edith of Scotland
William
d 1120
(drowned in the wreck of the 'White Ship')
Matilda
d 1167
m(i)
Henry V.
Holy Roman
Emperor
m(ii)
Geoffrey Plantagenet,
Count of Anjou
d 1151
Robert,
Earl of Glouce
d 1174
Henry II
d 1189
m Eleanor of Aquitaine
d 1204
William
died as a small child
1156
Henry
('The Young King')
m
Margaret of France
d 1183
(no issue)
Matilda
m
Henry ('The Lion'),
Duke of Saxony
Otto IV
Holy Roman Emperor
Richard
('Coeur de L
m
Berengaria o
(no issu
Geoffrey Plantagenet,
Archbishop of York
William Longsword,
Earl of Salisbury
(------- = illegitimate)

OF ENGLAND

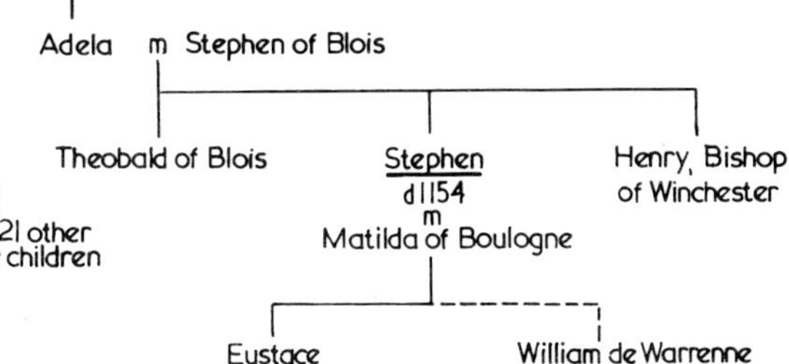

Adela m Stephen of Blois
Theobald of Blois
Stephen
d 1154
m
Matilda of Boulogne
Henry, Bishop
of Winchester
ast 21 other
nate children
Eustace
William de Warrenne

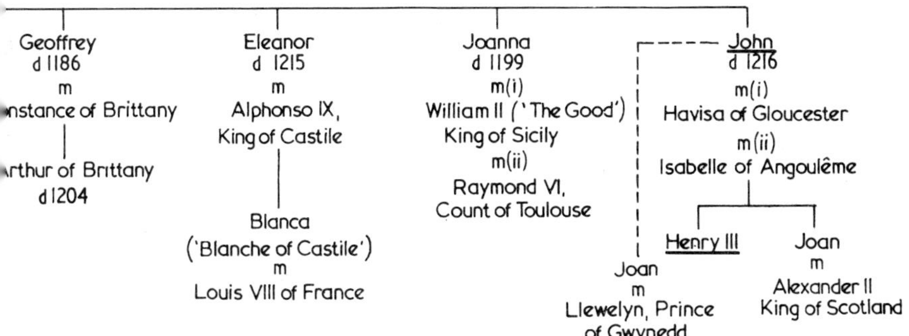

Geoffrey
d 1186
m
nstance of Brittany
rthur of Brittany
d 1204
Eleanor
d 1215
m
Alphonso IX,
King of Castile
Blanca
('Blanche of Castile')
m
Louis VIII of France
Joanna
d 1199
m(i)
William II ('The Good')
King of Sicily
m(ii)
Raymond VI,
Count of Toulouse
John
d 1216
m(i)
Havisa of Gloucester
m(ii)
Isabelle of Angoulême
Henry III
Joan
m
Alexander II
King of Scotland
Joan
m
Llewelyn, Prince
of Gwynedd

Author's Note

In the twelfth century Latin was the international language of religion, diplomacy, officialdom and scholarship. Churchmen, diplomats and scholars would often have conversed in Latin. The kings of France and their subjects, the Norman and Angevin kings of England, and Anglo–Norman aristocracy in England, talked French. The English speech of the ordinary people of England was still a foreign language or a second language to the descendants of the Norman conquerors. The subjects of Eleanor of Aquitaine spoke the *langue d'oc*, the language of the troubadours.

The dialogue in this book, whatever the language in which it originally took place, is given in modern English; but the author would like to stress that all the conversations were reported by contemporaries of the speakers, and none is fictitious.

Prologue: A Kingdom in Anarchy

> *. . . each man seized by a strange passion for violence, raged cruelly against his neighbour and reckoned himself the more glorious the more guiltily he attacked the innocent . . . So it was that none trod the King's highway untroubled as before, nor did man trust himself to man with the old confidence, but wherever one caught sight of another on the road his whole body straightway trembled and anxiously he shrank from view, either in a neighbouring wood or in some by-road . . .*
>
> (from *Gesta Stephani* – 'The Deeds of Stephen')

King Henry I, the youngest son of William the Conqueror, King of England and Duke of Normandy, spent a November day of 1135 hunting in the forest of Lyons.

After a day in the saddle, ignoring his doctor's advice, he rounded off his evening's pleasures with a huge helping of lampreys. They visited his stomach briefly and disagreed with him violently. The king was growing old and he was less tough than he seemed; a few days later he was dead.

Like his father William I – the bastard son of a Duke of Normandy, who conquered England in 1066 and became a king – Henry I was hard, unamiable and lucky. It was lucky for him that his elder brother William II – William Rufus – was homosexual: he had neither legitimate nor illegitimate children, which left Henry a clear path to the English throne. It was lucky for him that his eldest brother Robert, Duke of Normandy, lacked the strength to hold the continental inheritance which William the Conqueror had left him: forty years after the battle of Hastings Henry I reversed history and reconquered Normandy from his brother, thus reuniting the domains of William the Conqueror.

The ruthless Henry was in some respects a great king. His subjects called him Henry 'Beauclerc' because he was more literate than most laymen of his time, which made him a 'beau clerc' or good scholar in the eyes of the others. They also called him the 'Lion of Justice' because that was exactly what he was: a ruler with a leonine majesty and a ferocious passion to see justice done and order kept.

But luck and power were not proof against the ordinary limitations of mortality. Henry had at least twenty-one children, but only two of them were legitimate, a twin son and daughter named William and Matilda; and in 1120 William was drowned in mid-Channel, in one of the most famous shipwrecks of history, the loss of the *White Ship*.

Henry, however, was not left without an heir. Matilda was married to the Holy Roman Emperor Henry V, who died in 1125, leaving her as an available successor to her father's kingdom and duchy. At the beginning of 1127 Henry decided to nominate her as his heir, and he commanded his barons to take an oath of loyalty to her. They did so reluctantly, and only under the compulsion of King Henry's forceful temper.

As he lay on his deathbed, Henry may have doubted the wisdom of his decision. He had good reason to fear that his powerful, self-willed barons might not yield willingly to a woman's rule. He had three nephews, the sons of his sister Adela, and therefore the grandsons of William the Conqueror. Perhaps one of them would have been a better choice as his successor . . .

But it was too late to alter the provisions which he had already made; the barons' oath had been demanded and given years ago. On 1 December 1135, King Henry I died, leaving Matilda as his lawful successor, and his nephews as possibly preferable claimants. No great intelligence was required to see that the future was fraught with trouble, and not many years had passed before the people of England at least had begun to look back to the reign of the 'Lion of Justice' as a golden age.

In any kingdom of 'Christendom', as the community of Christian countries called itself, the king was the ruler of a country which was not a nation state but his own dynastic patrimony, the boundaries of which might alter from one generation to the next.

William the Conqueror had been at liberty to divide his lands to provide a kingdom for one son and a dukedom for another. Henry I's reuniting of those lands to the detriment of his brother had redefined the limits of his own power, but not the map of Christendom. As with the Anglo-Norman lands, so elsewhere: a kingdom might be partitioned by inheritance, or enlarged by conquest, diplomacy or marriage. But Christendom, from Ireland to Jerusalem and from Iceland to Sicily, was the frame which contained the fluctuating kingdoms.

In an ideal kingdom the king promulgated good laws, dispensed good justice and kept good order. He was assisted in his task by the grace of God, for his coronation was also a consecration, and if it did not make him a priest, it made him more than an ordinary layman. When he took Holy Communion he received both the bread and the wine like a priest, not the bread only like the rest of the laiety. In France and England, and possibly in other countries too, the king's subjects credited him with miraculous power, granted him by the special mandate of heaven, to heal or alleviate certain diseases.

Besides being a semi-sacred person, the king was an immensely powerful individual, theoretically the owner of every square foot of his kingdom, and the greatest lords were his tenants or 'vassals'. In return for their tenure of sometimes vast estates they owed the king services: good counsel in time of peace and military service in time of war. The king's great vassals were 'tenants-in-chief', and they in turn had their own vassals who owed them service. The whole structure was held together by the oath of 'homage' or loyalty, which each vassal paid to his lord or 'suzerain', and the military service paid by knight to lord and lord to king provided protection for the whole of society. Beneath the shield of this military hierarchy the ordinary people who worked the land and provided the bread of life for all, in return for their labours received protection and security.

The Church which crowned and consecrated the king for his task of ruling, sanctified every aspect of human life through its seven sacraments: ordination for priests who dispensed the other six; baptism for infants, confirmation and communion for all the faithful; matrimony to sanctify the unions of men and women; absolution for the repentant sinner; unction for the sick and dying. The Church tamed the aggressions of violent men, or directed them into holy courses, such as Crusades against the Infidel, and it taught the Christian virtues of love of God, humanity to one's fellowmen, and charity to the unfortunate.

Such was the ideal, but the reality fell far short of it, since ideal kingdoms have never existed beyond the boundaries of heaven, or of men's imaginations. Strong kings did their best, and under a king like Henry I the system of government briefly outlined above could work well enough. It has been labelled the 'feudal system' from the Latin *feudum* for 'fief' – the land which a vassal held in return for his homage and service.

Unfortunately the system was full of inherent anomalies, and from them sprang many of the situations which led to the strife, the tumult and the bitterness which occupied the reigns of the three kings with whom this book is chiefly concerned: King Henry II, King Richard I and King John.

The anomalies were explosive: the pope and his bishops, the king and his magnates, did not work hand in hand. Ecclesiastical authority and secular government indulged in unedifying struggles for supremacy in every kingdom. Vassalage was not as simple as it sounded in theory, for a king could hold lands in a neighbouring kingdom, and thereby became his neighbour's vassal for at least some of his lands. For instance, the King of Scots held lands in England, and the King of England held lands in France. Many lords and knights held fiefs from more than one suzerain, and where the oath of homage and the dictates of self-interest clashed, self-interest tended to emerge victorious. When churchmen, kings and lords warred with one another, the ordinary people were as helpless as the grains of corn crushed between two millstones. Oppression and violence were more likely to be the common experience of their daily lives than the protection and security which their lords were intended to provide.

Feudal society, like any other society, suffered to a constantly varying extent from the faults and failings of those who governed; but when there was an almost complete breakdown of government – as occurred after the death of Henry I – then the consequences were terrible indeed. The Peterborough Chronicler wrote:

> For every powerful man built his castles . . . and they filled the country full of castles. When the castles were built they filled them with devils and wicked men. Then, both by night and day, they took those people that they thought had any goods – men and women – and put them in prison and tortured them with indescribable tortures to extort gold and silver; for no martyrs were ever so tortured as they were. They were hung by the thumbs or by the head, and corselets were hung on their feet. Knotted ropes were put round their heads and twisted until they penetrated to the brains. They put them in prisons where there were adders and snakes and toads, and killed them like that. Some they put in a torture chamber – that is in a chest that was short, narrow and shallow, and they put sharp stones in it and pressed the man in it so that he had all his limbs broken. In many of the castles there was a 'noose-and-trap' – consisting of chains of such a kind that two or three men had enough to do to carry one. It was so made that it was fastened to a beam, and they used to put a sharp iron around the man's throat and his neck, so that he could not in any direction either sit or lie or sleep, but had to carry all that iron. Many thousands they killed by starvation . . . When the wretched people had no more to give, they robbed and burned all the villages, so that you could easily go a whole day's journey and never find anyone occupying a village, nor land tilled. The corn was dear, and meat and butter and cheese, because there was none in the country. Wretched people died of starvation; some lived by begging for alms, who had once been rich men; some fled the country.

Immediately after the death of Henry I it appeared that order would be maintained in England, though not in the way that Henry had intended.

Matilda was in Normandy when her father died, and one of the king's nephews, Stephen of Blois, outmanoeuvred her by making for England immediately and claiming the crown. The eldest of the three nephews, Theobald, might have done the same had he thought quickly enough, but he accepted Stephen's *fait accompli*. The youngest of the brothers, Henry of Blois, was ineligible for the throne, since he had entered the Church. As

Bishop of Winchester he was in England already, and he gave his support to Stephen. He secured for him the royal treasury, which was kept at Winchester, and later gained him recognition by the Papacy. Stephen was King of England by 22 December 1135, three weeks and one day after Henry I's death.

Stephen's action was not the clear case of usurpation that it now appears to have been. England had never had a woman ruler; succession by primogeniture had not yet been established; personal eligibility and membership of the royal house were respectable claims to kingship. On the other hand, Matilda was her father's chosen successor, and the recipient of the most solemn oath that the feudal world recognized, even if that oath was as frequently honoured in the breach as the observance.

Matilda was not the woman to see her rights flouted; furthermore, she had a son to inherit them. In 1128 Matilda had remarried. Her second husband was a powerful continental nobleman, Geoffrey Plantagenet, Count of Anjou, to whom, in 1133, she bore a son named Henry – the future King Henry II.

Territorially powerful Geoffrey Plantagenet might be, but the title of Countess of Anjou was not good enough for his wife. For the rest of her life Matilda continued to call herself Empress, and she was determined to become Queen of England if she could. Matilda was as ambitious and unamiable as her father, and she would probably have been a king in his own image if she had been a man; but as a woman fighting for her rights in a man's world she was at a disadvantage, and she lacked her father's luck.

It took Matilda some time to marshal her resources for an attack on Stephen. Geoffrey could do little to help her because many of Henry I's Norman vassals also held lands in England, and in order not to lose them they gave their allegiance to Stephen. So Geoffrey was faced with the prospect of re-conquering Normandy if his son were ever to inherit it. He accepted the challenge and fought inch by inch for his son's continental inheritance, while the boy's mother crossed the channel to do battle for the throne of England.

In 1139 Matilda invaded England with an army commanded by her half-brother, Robert, Earl of Gloucester, one of the numerous bastards of Henry I. Robert was no mean soldier, and for a time it appeared that Matilda's cause would triumph. Stephen was captured, and Matilda had herself proclaimed *Domina Anglorum* – 'Lady of the English' – the feminine form of the style *Dominus Anglorum* – 'Lord of the English' – which a king assumed after his accession and before his coronation.

Matilda, however, came no nearer to coronation than a solemn entry into London and the assumption of the title: the prosperous citizens who had welcomed Stephen, who claimed to have elected him king, and who dreaded the breakdown of law and order, had no welcome for Matilda. She was driven out of London, and shortly afterwards the soldiers of Bishop Henry of Winchester captured the Earl of Gloucester. The civil war, which for a moment looked as though it might have ended with a clear victory for

Matilda in 1141, was resumed when King Stephen and Earl Robert were released by an exchange agreement.

The consequence of the resumption of hostilities was the barbarism and desolation described by the Peterborough Chronicler, and the only statement which can be made to mitigate that pitiable description is that all of England did not suffer equally all the time. Most chronicles were written by members of monastic communities, each of whom could write with authority only of his own locality; even if he wrote of a man riding a whole day's journey and finding the same desolate conditions, he was still writing of a relatively limited area.

If any man could generalize with confidence it was probably the anonymous author of the *Gesta Stephani* – 'The Deeds of Stephen' – quoted at the beginning of this prologue. He may have been a clerk, or civil servant in holy orders, attached to Stephen's court. As he moved around the country in the wake of a king who vainly strove to impose order, he would have seen unhappy pattern of violence on the side of the powerful and miserable timidity on that of the helpless: a picture similar to that of the Peterborough Chronicler, though less exaggerated.

Although Stephen failed to impose order, his party in the main prevailed; nonetheless, Matilda did not despair. After her reverse in 1141 she seems to have made no further effort to secure the crown for herself, but rather to have fought to assert the future rights of her son. To this end, Count Geoffrey, still taken up with the affairs of Normandy and unable to visit England himself, sent over the nine-year-old Henry in 1142, principally to remind his partisans that support of Henry was an investment in the future.

Henry remained at the Early of Gloucester's headquarters at Bristol for almost two years, before it was deemed safer for him to return across the Channel. He paid a second visit to England in 1147, in nominal command of a military expedition which met with such total disaster that Stephen paid Henry's passage home. Stephen was always humane, but if his generosity was also intended to express his dismissive attitude to his enemies it was a mistaken gesture, even though Robert of Gloucester had died and Matilda retired to Normandy never to return.

Henry Plantagenet's third expedition to England, and his first personal attempt to win the throne, took place in 1149. The seriousness of his purpose was illustrated at the outset by his seeking the honour of knighthood from King David I of Scotland, who was his great-uncle on his mother's side. In the twelfth century it was not customary for a father to knight his son, the reason being to ensure that knighthood was conferred for merit and not for favour. So Henry made the long journey to Carlisle to be knighted by the most exalted of his relations, and then marched south, no longer an ambitious youth but a fully-fledged warrior.

A few minor successes gave promise of Henry's developing military ability, but he lacked the resources and the experience to defeat Stephen, who was a capable soldier, if not a successful ruler. Henry returned once more to Normandy at the beginning of 1150, to leave Stephen a brief interlude of peace as his reign drew to its close.

In 1135 Stephen had seized the advantage of that '. . . tide in the affairs of men which, taken at the flood, leads on to fortune'. Fifteen years later he may have realized that it had turned against him; it was running in Henry Plantagenet's favour, and would presently sweep him in turn on to the throne of England. But in the meantime Henry had other ambitions to pursue, among them marriage with a queen who might fairly claim to be the most famous woman in Christendom.

PART ONE

King Henry II

Just as the thirty five years of his reign contain a concentration of the human condition, so his character covers a vast field of human nature. He was simple and royal . . . direct and paradoxical, compassionate and hard, a man of intellect, a man of action. God-fearing, superstitious, blasphemous, far-seeing, short sighted, affectionate, lustful, patient, volcanic, humble, overriding. It is difficult to think of any facet of man which at some time he didn't demonstrate, except chastity and sloth.

(Christopher Fry, *Curtmantle*, Preface)

I
Henry Plantagenet

Ecce advenit Dominator Dominus; et regnum in manu eiius, et potestas, et imperium (*Behold he comes, the Lord our Governor, and in his hand is royal power and might.*)

(Introit for the Mass of Epiphany)

The parents of Henry Plantagenet were strongly contrasted characters, and a singularly ill-assorted married couple; it was small wonder that their son was a complex and inconsistent personality.

The Empress Matilda, whose pride was considered disproportionate even in an age when pride was the expected concommitant of greatness, was imperial by marriage and royal on both sides of her family. Through her father she inherited the blood of the Norman conqueror of England, through her mother the older royalty of Anglo-Saxon England and of Scotland. Henry I's queen had been Edith of Scotland, the daughter of King Malcolm III and his wife St Margaret, who was the grand-daughter of the Saxon king, Edmund Ironside. It was scarcely surprising that Matilda was not content to take the title of countess when she married her second husband.

Geoffrey Plantagenet was not royal, but the ruling family of Anjou claimed an ancestry more awesome than that of any human royalty. The Angevins believed that they were descended from Melusine, the daughter of Satan. The family legend was that one of the earlier Counts of Anjou, Fulk Nerra or Fulk the Black, had gone on a journey and returned from his unknown destination with a wife of surpassing beauty. The Countess Melusine bore her husband four children, and made him an admirable consort in every way but one: in an age of piety she seldom attended Mass, and whenever she did so, she made sure to leave before the consecration of the bread and wine. This was highly suspect behaviour, and at last Fulk reluctantly ordered four of his knights to hold Melusine in her place the next time she attempted to leave Mass. The result was dramatic: the knights obeyed their lord, but Melusine tore herself free of them and flew out of the window of the church, carrying two of her children away with her. So her identity was revealed, for no devil can endure to look upon the consecrated Body and Blood of Christ. However, in her escape, Melusine had left two children behind, to provide a human link between the house of Anjou and Hell itself.

The most unfortunate consequence of this legend was that the Angevins believed that any violent acts which they chose to commit were the inevitable consequences of being descendants of the Devil: hysterical rages, atrocities perpetrated in blind fury, sexual excesses, all were inescapable legacies from Satan.

It is quite possible that Count Geoffrey nourished his family legend to counterbalance the formidable regality of his wife. He certainly needed some means to assert himself, for at the time of their marriage Matilda was twenty-five and Geoffrey scarcely fifteen. When they married he was in fact only the heir to Anjou, which made his inferiority to his wife yet more obvious; but almost at once he came into his inheritance, for his father Count Fulk V married the widowed Queen Melisande of Jerusalem. Fulk resigned his hereditary lands to his son, and rode away to rule the Crusader kingdom in right of his new wife, leaving the young Geoffrey lord of the vast domains of Anjou, and of Maine which he had inherited from his mother Ermentrude, the daughter of Count Hélias of Maine. Thus it was that the empress' satanically descended boy husband suddenly became a king's son and a mighty lord in his own right; and since he had inherited the violent temper and the lust for power which characterized his family it is unlikely that he remained his wife's subordinate for long.

His acquisition of the surname Plantagenet was characteristically out of the ordinary. Count Geoffrey, in common with most noblemen of his time, was passionately fond of hunting. Desirous of improving the game coverts in his forests, he planted thickets of broom all over his domains. The Latin name of broom is *Planta genesta*, and somebody, amused by the young count's enthusiasm for it, nicknamed him Geoffrey 'Plantagenet' or Geoffrey 'broom plant'. Perhaps in response to the jest he took to decorating his helmet with a sprig of the brilliant yellow flowers of the broom. In time it was adopted as a family emblem, and Count Geoffrey's nickname, handed on to his descendants, became one of the most resonant surnames of history.

Geoffrey and Matilda had three sons: the birth of Henry in 1133 was followed by that of Geoffrey in 1134 and of William in 1136. Count Geoffrey was determined to give his sons a good education, for high intelligence and respect for scholarship characterized the house of Anjou as clearly as did the love of sport and war and the indulgence of savage temper. Count Geoffrey had once ordered that the Bishop and canons of Séez, who had presumed to defy his authority, should be castrated; yet he was in touch with the leading intellectuals of his day, and he knew where to find the most pretigious tutors for his eldest son.

The young Henry's first tutor was a renowned scholar and poet, Peter of Saintes. During his stay at Bristol, at the court of Earl Robert of Gloucester, Henry knew and probably learned much from the brilliant and widely travelled Adelard of Bath, who played a great part in transmitting the learning of the Moslem world to Western Europe. After his return to Normandy his tutor was William of Conches, a scholar whose reputation by no means lagged behind that of his predecessors. It was natural enough, therefore, that in later life Henry appreciated the company of literary men, and that his court was a centre of intelligent patronage.

Henry Plantagenet served a demanding apprenticeship both in learning and in war. After his third expedition to England had ended in failure – but in honourable and promising failure – Count Geoffrey, who had conquered Normandy on his behalf, and had latterly ruled it as regent for him, solemnly resigned the rule of the great duchy to Henry, in 1150. This transaction led inexorably to the performance of another solemn ceremony: the homage of the Duke of Normandy to the King of France, for, despite the wealth and power of its dukes, Normandy was a fief of the French crown.

It was remarkable in a family notorious for power lust, for ambition and territorial greed, that Count Geoffrey possessed the policy and the generosity to hand over the fruits of his conquest to his eldest son. But he was well aware that as an Angevin he was disliked on grounds of racial prejudice in Normandy; whereas Henry, with his inheritance of Norman blood, did not suffer the same disadvantage.

In August 1151 Count Geoffrey and his eldest son rode to Paris, where Henry was to offer his homage to the King of France. Count Geoffrey was then thirty-eight years old, and Henry was seventeen. Geoffrey was known as Geoffrey the Fair, or the Handsome; he was clever, eccentric, and in the prime of life. Henry had inherited his father's violent temper and his intellectual vivacity, but not his striking good looks. Superficially Henry was less attractive, but he could charm both men and women when he chose. He probably resembled his Norman forebears, William the Conqueror and his sons: he had their bright red-gold hair, their muscular build and their majesty of presence.

The king to whom the young Henry Plantagenet owed his homage was Louis VII, a king who was regarded as a pattern of knighthood: a crusader, a brave warrior, and a man both courteous and guileless. His sense of honour often put him at a disadvantage in political dealings with men less scrupulous than himself, but his personal prestige was immense. He was also deeply religious, which increased the respect with which he was regarded, for he lived in an age when all kings acted with outward piety but few attempted genuine Christian conduct.

Louis' queen was one of the most brilliant women of her century, perhaps one of the most vivid feminine personalities of any century: Eleanor of Aquitaine, whose long career as the wife of two kings and the mother of three, spans almost the whole of the period included in this book.

A contemporary described Queen Eleanor as *perpulchra*, which may be translated as 'more than beautiful'. All who saw her unanimously praised her beauty; but tantalizingly, none described her. Her most distinguished biographer has suggested that she was almost certainly fair in colouring, because white skin and golden hair were essential ingredients in the medieval ideal of beauty. Her effigy in the Abbey of Fontevrault shows her as tall and slender. Medieval effigies were intended as stylized images of king, queen or knight – almost as chessmen are today – rather than as portraits of individuals; but Eleanor is probably correctly represented as tall and slender, for even in late middle age she could successfully disguise herself as a man, and mere mischance, not womanly curves, betrayed her. All her life she displayed vital intelligence, unstable in youth and unswervingly purposeful as she grew older. Mental and physical vigour remained with her until she was over eighty years old. It could have been said of her as of Shakespeare's Cleopatra 'age cannot wither her'. It has not done so yet.

Louis and Eleanor had been married since 1137, and for many years thereafter the King of France had adored his wife to an extent that was unkindly described as 'almost puerile'. But many stresses had eroded their relationship: all those years of marriage had produced only two daughters, Marie and Alix, not the necessary male heir to the throne of France. There was also the profound difference of temperament between the king and queen: Louis' intense seriousness and piety paired uneasily with Eleanor's ardent *joie de vivre*, much as it fascinated and charmed him.

The sombre and penitential aspects of Louis' religious life increased after the unhappy incident of Vitry-le-Brulé – 'Vitry-the-Burned' – in 1143. In one of those outbreaks of private warfare in which a king with powerful vassals was constantly called upon to intervene, some of the royal troops had burned the church in the town of Vitry, in which thirteen hundred people had taken refuge. A church normally provided the right of sanctuary, or protection from violence or forcible removal. But the king's troops were *routiers*, mercenaries who had little respect for the sanctions of the church, which were indeed as unpredictably observed or disregarded as those of the Geneva Convention. The screams of the thirteen hundred people burned to death in the church of Vitry re-echoed in Louis' conscience until his dying day, although he had not ordered the sack of the town, and would have prevented its consequences if he could. Eleanor, who did not hold her husband guilty, had little patience with his burdened conscience; his self-inflicted austerities caused her to remark that she seemed to be married to a monk, not to a king.

However, in 1146 when Louis resolved to go on crusade to the Holy Land, in response to the fervent preaching of St Bernard of Clairvaux, Eleanor also 'took the Cross' – that is, she committed herself to make the journey to Jerusalem, and wore a cross embroidered on her mantle, in token of her vow. Whether as unarmed pilgrims or as members of military expeditions, many women took the Cross together with their menfolk; but the journey was arduous and dangerous, and many left their bones in the Near East, while some were captured and sold into slavery. Though the Queen of France could expect to travel with greater comfort and safety than other women, her impulse to take the Crusader's vow was nonetheless both pious and courageous.

In 1144 the Christian fortress of Edessa had been captured by the Turks, and a rising tide of Moslem conquest threatened the very existence of the kingdom of Jerusalem, the foundation of which had been the successful outcome of the First Crusade, half a century earlier. Its king was now Baldwin III, Geoffrey Plantagenet's half-brother, the son of King Fulk and Queen Melisande. He was only a boy, and it was obvious that if the Christians were to remain in possession of the Holy Places, he needed help from the west.

There was always a trickle of crusaders – devout pilgrims and adventurous knights – *en route* for the Holy Land. The Second Crusade of 1147 was so named because it was the second general summons to all the knighthood of Christendom. Both the King of France and the Holy Roman Emperor Conrad of Hohenstaufen responded to the call of Pope Eugenius III to go to the defence of Jerusalem.

The events of the Crusade lie beyond the scope of this book, except insofar as they served to alienate the King and Queen of France. As Duchess of Aquitaine Eleanor commanded her own vassals, although their ultimate suzerain was the King of France. It was one of Eleanor's vassals, Geoffrey de Rancon, who was leading the advance guard of the French army when it was ambushed by the Turks on the pass over Mount Cadmos. At the time it was believed that Geoffrey de Rancon had been advancing upon the orders of Eleanor and not of Louis, whose personal bravery alone averted defeat. Then, when the Crusaders reached Antioch in 1148, Eleanor sought light relief from the rigours of the journey in an indiscreet flirtation with her handsome young uncle, Raymond of Poitiers, who ruled as Prince of Antioch – just as Fulk had ruled as King of Jerusalem – in right of his wife, Constance.

The Crusade failed in its main objective, a decisive repulse of the advancing Turks, though Jerusalem remained in Christian hands for the present. King Louis VII returned to France accompanied by the double humiliation of military failure and the rumoured infidelity of his queen.

Eleanor was supposed at one time or another to have indulged in scandalous affairs with a remarkable variety of men, including Raymond of Poitiers, Saldebreuil de Sanzay, the Constable of Aquitaine, the troubadour Marcabru – whom Louis VII had ordered to leave the French court – and Geoffrey Plantagenet. Yet Eleanor was probably more notorious than she deserved. Doubtless she was a woman who could not resist testing the effect of her charm on any susceptible man; but far more significant than all the gossip is the fact that nobody ever questioned the legitimacy of any of her ten children.

When Geoffrey and Henry Plantagenet arrived at the French court the marriage of Louis and Eleanor was what would now be described as on the rocks. The young Henry must have gazed with the most ardent interest at the beautiful and notorious queen, whose name gossip linked with that of his father. What he could not possibly have known – it would have seemed beyond imagination – was that he was looking at his own future wife.

Before Henry gave his homage for Normandy to King Louis there was some unpleasantness to be settled.

For reasons of temporary relevance Count Geoffrey had made war upon and captured one Giraud Berlai, a vassal of the King of France, and he brought him to the French court in chains. Geoffrey had been excommunicated for attacking the vassal of an absent Crusader, but he was completely unrepentant for Giraud had evidently caused him deep offence.

Bernard of Clairvaux offered to resolve the matter. The ascetic Cistercian abbot who had preached the Second Crusade was one of the most influential ecclesiastics of the twelfth century, and was regarded as a saint in his own lifetime. He offered to absolve Geoffrey from his excommunication if he would set Giraud free.

Excommunication was the formal severing of a man from the Christian community, and was held to condemn him to eternal damnation should he die unabsolved. But the descendants of Melusine were not afraid of such a fate. Geoffrey answered St Bernard with characteristic Angevin violence:

'I refuse to free my captive, and if it is a sin to hold a prisoner then I refuse to be absolved of that sin.'

St Bernard replied with mild menace:

'Beware, Count of Anjou, with what measure ye mete it shall be meted unto you.'

For answer, Count Geoffrey stormed out of the room.

Quite suddenly, a few days later, Geoffrey released Giraud Berlai, and Henry, who had withheld his homage until the trouble had been resolved, performed it with a good grace. The court buzzed with rumour: some people said Geoffrey's change of front was the delayed result of St Bernard's words; some said Queen Eleanor had used her charm on Geoffrey; or perhaps she had used it on Henry, and induced him to persuade his father . . .

The Plantagenets left Paris and rode homewards to their own domains through the scorching days of late summer. On the way Count Geoffrey decided to take a swim in an invitingly cold river. That evening he was sweating and shivering with a fever; a few days later he was dead.

During the following months dramatic events happened in such rapid sequence that the gossip-mongers of Christendom had scarcely time to keep one another informed.

Henry Plantagenet through the sudden death of his father, became Duke of Normandy and Count of Anjou and Maine, the lord of a vast tract of territory, surpassing in area the lands directly ruled by the King of France. Those lords who had fought for his mother the Empress Matilda called him not Henry Plantagenet but Henry 'FitzEmpress': in their eyes the son of the empress and the great-grandson of the Conqueror was the lawful heir of England. Henry himself held the same opinion, and it would not be long before he made a new attempt to assert his claim.

In the meantime the crisis in the relationship of the King and Queen of France reached its conclusion. During the autumn of 1151 the administration of France and Aquitaine was carefully disentangled: vassals of Louis who had command of castles in Aquitaine were systematically replaced by vassals of Eleanor.

On 21 March 1152 the marriage of Louis and Eleanor was dissolved by the Archbishop of Sens and a synod of clergy, on the grounds of consanguinity. This meant that the royal couple was related within the 'forbidden degrees' of kinship. It is still impossible for people who are very closely related to be married in church, but in the twelfth century the prohibition extended to remote cousins; and, since most of the royal families of Christendom were related, a papal dispensation, or exceptional permission, was almost always required for a royal marriage. Louis and Eleanor were very distantly related, so distantly that a dispensation had not been sought. But lack of one provided acceptable grounds for an annulment.

Eleanor of Aquitaine was extremely fortunate that her husband was prepared to submit to this official procedure. Had Louis VII been less honourable, had he chosen to accuse his queen of adultery and produce false witnesses to attest her guilt, he could have had her burned to death, and then claimed the Duchy of Aquitaine as forfeit of the queen – the adultery of a queen being regarded as treason to the royal blood because it made questionable the legitimacy of the royal issue.

But, since Louis VII was, in the opinion of one writer on the period, 'with the exception of his great-grandson St Louis IX, probably the most noble hero who has ever held the throne of France', he did not push his advantage to the ultimate limits, even though the annulment of his marriage depleted the area directly under his control by a vast tract of territory which extended from the Pyrenees to the boundaries of the Île de France. The patrimony of Louis VII was the Île de France, and the great fiefs which made up the area which we now call France enjoyed considerable independence although they acknowledged Louis' suzerainty. His power as King of France depended on his personal prestige; that his power was great was his measure as a man.

Freed from her husband, Eleanor rode south to Poitiers, the capital of her duchy, a reigning duchess without a knightly protector. Melisande of Jerusalem and Constance of Antioch had previously found themselves in a similarly vulnerable position. Eleanor realized, as they had done, that it behoved her to acquire a powerful husband to defend her possessions . . .

Eleanor of Aquitaine made haste to offer her hand in marriage to Henry of Normandy, Anjou and Maine.

Not only did his vast inheritance make Henry already the most eligible bachelor in Christendom, but he possessed an excellent chance of becoming the King of England. Like the Empress Matilda, Eleanor did not relish the prospect of exchanging a greater title for a lesser.

Henry Plantagenet and Eleanor of Aquitaine were married in the cathedral of Poitiers on 18 May 1152. Thence forward their conjoint domains extended from the southern boundary of Aquitaine to the Norman coast, and their conjoint resources were at Henry's disposal for the conquest of England.

Nothing in the circumstances of their marriage suggests a love match. Indeed, marrying for love was contrary to the custom of the age; the marriages of great persons were arranged to provide political alliances and to unite kingdoms or fiefs. But though there was a disparity of eleven years in their ages, Eleanor was a famous beauty and Henry a virile young man with a strong appreciation of lovely women; it is probable that sexual ardour seasoned a union based upon shared ambition.

Soon after his marriage Henry began his preparations to claim the kingdom which he regarded as his lawful inheritance. With the wealth of Aquitaine to finance an expedition far greater than any which his mother's partisans had been able to despatch, he landed in England early in 1153.

It was 6 January, the feast of Epiphany, the day on which the Three Kings had come to adore the infant Jesus. As was customary on a Holy Day, Henry attended Mass, entering the first church which he saw on English ground. As he went in, the priest was chanting the Introit, and Henry heard the opening words of the Mass of Epiphany: *Ecce advenit Dominator Dominus. et regnum in manu eiius, et potestas, et imperium* – 'Behold he comes, the Lord our Governor, and in his hand is royal power and might.'

Few men could have failed to experience a lift of the heart at so good an omen. Its promise was rapidly fulfilled. King Stephen was ageing, and wearied with the struggle to maintain even the shadow of authority. In the face of a new invasion he offered to treat for peace. Two churchmen came forward to act as mediators: Henry, Bishop of Winchester, the king's brother, and Theobald, Archbishop of Canterbury. The latter was ably assisted by his protégé, an ambitious cleric named Thomas Becket.

King Stephen's son Eustace, a competent soldier, but a man unpopular for his brutality, retaliated to the prospect of losing his inheritance by ravaging Archbishop Theobald's estates. In the opinion of contemporaries it was by the judgment of God that he suddenly fell sick and died, leaving Stephen without a direct heir.

At a council at Winchester in 1153 an agreement was reached whereby Stephen accepted Henry Plantagenet as his successor: his one immutable condition was that he should remain King of England for the rest of his life. From Winchester Henry and Stephen rode to London, to be greeted by the cheers of the populace, who saw in the prospect of a peaceful succession the promise of an ending to the long torment of the years of anarchy.

The succession arranged, Henry returned to Normandy, to see the child which Eleanor had borne him during the summer of 1153. As though the fates had conspired to offer insult to the King of France, the first child of Eleanor and Henry, so swiftly conceived, was a son. He was given the name of William, which had belonged both to kings of England and dukes of Aquitaine.

One triumph followed another. Next year, on 25 October, King Stephen died. The news was brought to Normandy early in November; exactly a year after his treaty with Stephen, Henry Plantagenet succeeded to the English throne.

Despite the wild resistance of the weather, Henry and Eleanor, accompanied by Henry's brothers and by many lords, struggled in storm-tossed vessels across the Channel. On 19 December 1154, in Westminster Abbey, Archbishop Theobald crowned them King and Queen of England.

Kingship and Government

The sacred character of kingship is symbolically illustrated by this mosaic of William II 'The Good', King of Sicily, being crowned by Christ, from the Cathedral of Monreale (MANSELL COLLECTION)

The coronation of King Henry I. The presence of the officiating bishops and the ritual of the coronation stress the theory that the King's power was derived from God and bestowed on him through the medium of the Church (RADIO TIMES HULTON PICTURE LIBRARY)

Henry II disputing with Thomas Becket. Despite the theoretically co-operative relations between sacred and secular authority, unseemly religio-political power struggles frequently occurred. The long battle between Henry and Becket was a single, though extreme, example (PICTUREPOINT)

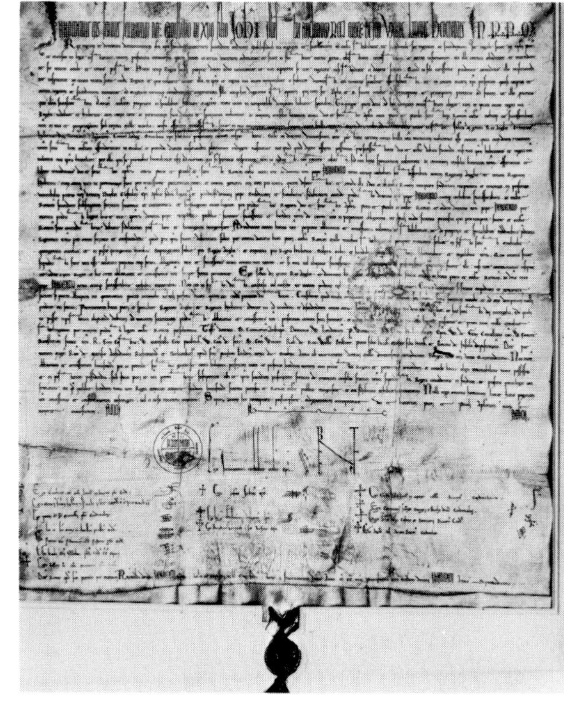

The Bull of Pope Innocent III, accepting King John's acknowledgement of the Pope as his suzerain, and of England as a fief of the Holy See. The event here recorded was in reality one of political rather than of religious significance; it did not represent, as it appears to do, a triumph of sacred over secular authority (BRITISH MUSEUM)

The king as ruler: King John enthroned, an illustration of the symbolic power of kingship as the source of justice, order and good government. The King was personally responsible for initiating and organizing every aspect of government throughout his kingdom of England and his continental fiefs (PICTUREPOINT)

A royal instrument of government: part of the Charter Roll of the reign of King John. It records grants of property made by the King under his Great Seal (PUBLIC RECORD OFFICE)

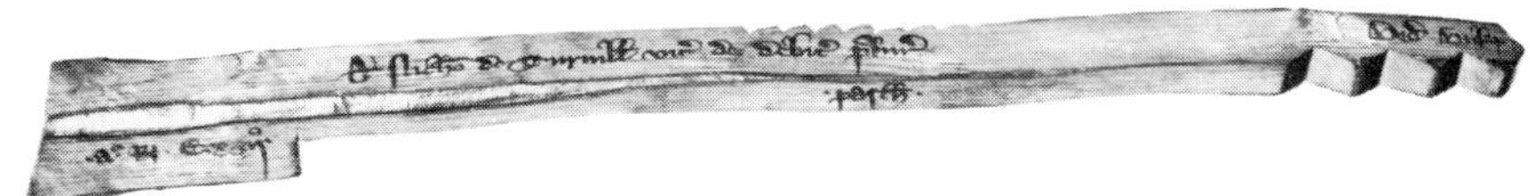

A remote ancestor of the computer: exchequer tallies used in calculating the royal accounts (PUBLIC RECORD OFFICE)

A fourteenth-century representation of judges (above) *and prisoners* (below). *The reign of Henry II saw the establishment at Westminster of the bench of judges which eventually became the Court of Common Pleas* (MANSELL COLLECTION)

The king as soldier:
The medieval king was expected to be his own commander-in-chief, and to be personally a renowned warrior. The dangers attendant upon the heroic concept of kingship are illustrated by the representation of Philip Augustus of France being unhorsed at the battle of Bouvines (1214) (RADIO TIMES HULTON PICTURE LIBRARY)

In fact, kings were rarely killed in battle, because of their high value as political hostages or ransomable prisoners. Richard Coeur-de-Lion and Mercadier reconnoitre the castle of Chaluz: the exception proves the rule, for this small-scale siege led directly to Richard's death (PICTUREPOINT)

The king at leisure:

King John hunting. The chase was the favourite relaxation of the Plantagenet kings, and the royal forests, or hunting preserves, covered a large area of England, in which beasts of the chase were protected by stringent laws (BRITISH LIBRARY)

A king and queen feasting, entertained by a musician. Though hunting and feasting provided welcome contrasts to the rigours of responsibility, intellectual pleasures were not despised by the Plantagenet kings. Henry II enjoyed the company of scholars; Richard I composed poetry; King John travelled his kingdom well supplied with books (BRITISH MUSEUM)

The possessions of royalty;

The regalia comprised the symbols of kingly power. At his coronation the king was crowned, annointed, and invested with the other items of his regalia. The Imperial Orb (left), *symbolic of the heavenly rule of Christ and the earthly supremacy of the emperor* (KUNSTHISTORISCHES MUSEUM, VIENNA)

Not all the splendid possessions of a king were symbolic. The 'King John Cup' (right), *one of the few items of King John's treasure which was not lost in the quicksands of the Wellstream; a lidded cup, exquisitely enamelled, and intended for daily use at the royal table* (COLIN SHEWRING)

The most famous document of King John's reign: the peace signed between King John and his rebellious subjects on 15 June, 1215, later known as Magna Carta, and ultimately apotheosized as the 'palladium of English liberties' (BRITISH MUSEUM)

The scene of the birth of a legend: 'The meadow that is called Runnymede between Windsor and Staines', where the historic document was signed (A. F. KERSTING)

II
Master of an Empire

> Marshal *Memory is not so harsh as the experience. Who can recall now the full devastation of the time when young Henry Plantagenet first came into his Kingdom? . . . Up and down the land he went, sparing neither himself nor us who were hauled along after him. Order was being born out of the sweat of those days and nights . . .*
>
> (Christopher Fry, *Curtmantle*, Prologue)

The importance of England in the eyes of its Norman kings and their Angevin successors was that it made them the 'peers' or equals of the kings of France. William the Conqueror and his descendants continued to pay homage to the kings of France for their lands on the French side of the Channel; but the conquest of the southern half of Britain had conferred on them the kingship which made them in feudal terms the equals of their continental suzerains, or of any other kings in Christendom. This was the basis of Henry Plantagenet's determination to press his claim to the throne of England; otherwise, the responsibility of governing Normandy, Anjou, Maine and Aquitaine might have seemed enough for him. But 'enough' was probably not a word which had much meaning for Henry, unless it were to complain that there was never enough time for all that he had to do.

When Henry became King of England at the age of twenty-one, he had matured into a very formidable man. All who saw him were impressed by his leonine appearance and his aura of physical and intellectual power. It was said that apart from sitting astride a horse he seldom sat down except to eat. He was ceaselessly on the move, and he adopted a costume which suited his active life – a tunic and hose and a short riding cloak. His English barons, who dressed conservatively in the long robes of the Anglo–Norman aristocracy called him Henry 'Curtmantle' ('shortcloak'); it was an age with a passion for nicknames some of which, like 'Plantagenet' itself, proved to be surnames in the making.

King Henry wore out his courtiers and servants with his dynamic energy. Peter of Blois, who was one of his intimates, wrote an amusing account of what he and the rest of them had to endure:

> If the King had promised to remain in a place for that day – and especially if he had announced his intention publicly by the mouth of a herald – he is sure to upset all the arrangements by departing early in the morning. As a result, you see men dashing around as if they were mad, beating their packhorses, running their carts into one another – in short, giving a lively imitation of Hell. If, on the other hand, the King orders an early start, he is certain to change his mind, and you can take it for granted that he will sleep until midday. Then you will see the packhorses loaded and waiting, the carts prepared, the courtiers dozing, traders fretting and everyone grumbling . . . When our couriers had gone ahead almost the whole day's ride, the King would turn aside to some other place where he had, it might be, just a single house with accommodation for himself and no one else. I hardly dare say it, but I believe that in truth he took a delight in seeing what a fix he put us in. After wandering some three or four miles in an unknown wood; and often in the dark, we thought ourselves lucky if we stumbled upon some filthy little hovel. There was often a sharp and bitter argument about a mere hut, and swords were drawn for possession of a lodging which pigs would have shunned.

Profoundly exasperating Henry undoubtedly was; yet in Peter of Blois' account of his unpredictable lifestyle there is an affectionate undertone. It was one of the many paradoxes of Henry's character that he could inspire devotion in his servants, though in the end he alienated every member of his family. From the beginning of his reign it was obvious that he was an impossible master, and yet an excellent one, who knew how to make men work for him. That he would prove an intolerable husband and father, who could love and be unloved, was a fact which belonged to the future.

Henry II did not live a life of ceaseless activity merely out of personal restlessness; his presence was constantly demanded throughout his domains, in places many miles apart. A man who was personally responsible for law, order and administration from the Cheviots to the Pyrenees had to ride far and fast. It was a compliment to his dedication to the task that Louis VII remarked that the King of England moved so fast that he seemed to fly rather than to ride.

After his coronation Henry gave his immediate attention to England, where he conceived it his first task to heal the wounds of the anarchy. He saw himself as the successor of his grandfather, Henry I; he would have liked to relegate the reign of Stephen to the condition of a forgotten episode.

He issued a Coronation Charter, as Henry I and Stephen had done, but he did not give the customary promise to honour the grants made by his predecessor; he promised to honour the *status quo* of 1135, the date of Henry I's death. This meant that all who had received titles, lands and privileges from Stephen were dependent for their renewal on Henry II's favour. Henry II repossessed some of the domains of the Crown which Stephen had granted away, but he did not push the implications of his charter to extremities. Probably it was intended principally as propaganda to suggest that Stephen had exercised the rights of the Crown as a usurper.

Having defined his position in unmistakably strong terms, Henry progressed to action. He ordered the destruction of all castles illegally built during Stephen's reign: the strongholds of the local tyrants whose activities the Peterborough Chronicler described. The number of illegal strongholds destroyed has been set as high as 1,115; but whatever the number, when the destruction was completed, one castle in five, throughout the country, belonged to the king.

Equally influential in the restoration of peace was the expulsion of the Flemish mercenaries who had nominally served King Stephen, but who had grown so undisciplined that they were scarcely better than brigands. Save for a few, who settled on the Welsh Marches, where there was official peace but enough unofficial trouble to keep them busy, they disappeared from the country 'as phantoms vanish', leaving it the quieter for their absence.

Only a few of Stephen's erstwhile supporters resisted Henry, and the most recalcitrant had yielded by the summer of 1155. Yet despite the firmness of his measures to write off the past and to stamp out disorder, Henry II did not refuse the services of able state officials merely because they were associated with the reign of his predecessor. He prized ability, and those who were prepared to serve the king loyally, though the crown had been transferred from one head to another, were welcomed by him. He took over Stephen's two justiciars, Robert, Earl of Leicester and Richard de Lucy, and Stephen's treasurer, Nigel, Bishop of Ely.

Without oversimplification, it is difficult to describe the tasks of these great officials. The Justiciars were in effect the king's immediate deputies, who might be granted powers of regency, or appointed to act as regents in conjunction with the queen while the king was abroad. The office of treasurer sounds self-explanatory, yet each of the great officials of state was expected to be able to act in almost any capacity that the king might require: judicial, administrative, financial or military. But Henry II expected no more of his officials than he was prepared to perform himself: he had an excellent head for figures; he was a tireless administrator; the legal system of this country still owes something to the influence of his ideas; and he was a more than competent soldier, though it was said to his credit that in warfare he grieved at the waste of human life more than he rejoiced at victory. He was omnicompetent, and he valued the same quality in others.

He found what he valued in the new chancellor whom he appointed the month after his coronation: Thomas Becket, Archdeacon of Canterbury, whose skill in diplomacy had first been displayed before him at the Council of Winchester in 1153.

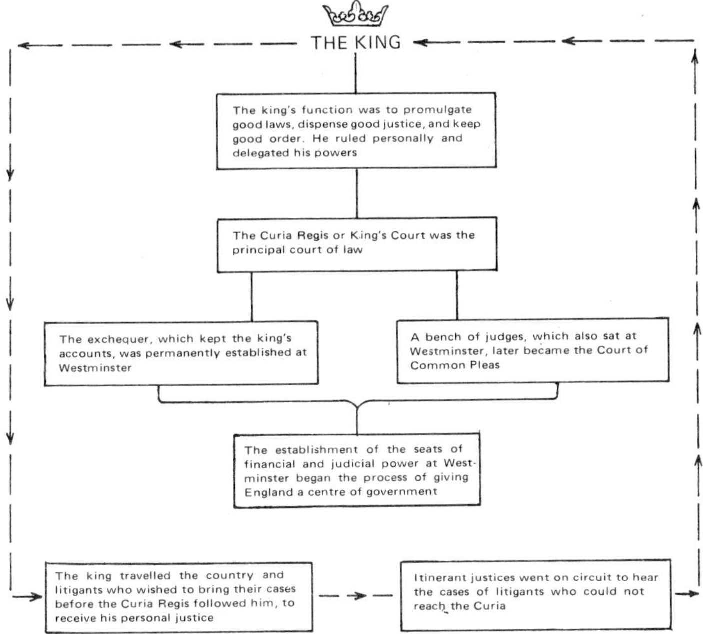

Diagram illustrating the role of the King as the source of justice in the reign of Henry II. The judgments of the Curia Regis, of the King's courts (which were still judicial committees of the Curia) and the itinerant justices, made up the body of 'case law', the precedents which created the English Common Law. Henry II, in a series of 'Assizes', or royal decrees given in an assize or solemn session of King and Counsellors, greatly extended the scope of royal justice, thereby undermining the power of the Church courts and of local feudal jurisdictions.

Becket was of Norman stock, the son of a citizen of London. He had been educated at the Augustinian priory of Merton with the intention that he should enter the Church, and he had spent his holdiays from Merton in the household of an aristocratic friend of his family, Richer de l'Aigle. There he had learnt the knightly skills of horsemanship, jousting, hawking and hunting, which fitted him for courtly society despite his relatively humble origins. As the protégé of Archbishop Theobald he had been appointed Archdeacon of Canterbury, a principally administrative position in the Church, which did not necessitate ordination as a priest.

When he became Chancellor of England Thomas Becket was not ordained. His way of life was secular, and as chancellor he kept a household of exceptional magnificence. In the midst of it all, however, he himself lived a life of frugality and chastity; personally he was a natural ascetic, though he loved outward show.

Becket was fourteen years older than the king, but despite the difference in their ages and in their characters a warm friendship grew between them. They complemented each other: Becket burned with ambition, and Henry could fulfil it; Becket had brilliant ability, and Henry could employ it. Common absorption in the demanding and satisfying tasks of government bound them together, and during their hours of leisure they indulged a shared passion for hawking and hunting. Throughout Becket's years as chancellor their partnership was close and constructive.

When Henry had set England on the road to recovery he turned his attention to his continental domains. Throughout 1156 Henry made the weight of his hand felt wherever it was needed, beginning with the lands of his patrimony, and later in the year entering Aquitaine which he had scarcely visited since his marriage.

Aquitaine was notorious for its disorderliness, its ceaseless internecine feuds which neither its native rulers nor their suzerains the kings of France had ever been able to control. But though Aquitaine was a cauldron of troubles, it was also the nursery of the Cult of Courtly Love, and the home of its literary exponents, the troubadours.

Writing in the *langue d'oc*, the southern variant of French which gave its name to a whole region, the troubadours celebrated *amor de lonh* ('the love of one remote'), the worship of an unattainable yet not indifferent lady. At one extreme Courtly Love was almost religious in the veneration which the poet offered to his lady, and it was perhaps akin to the cult of the Virgin Mary, which was playing an increasing part in the religious life of the time. At the other extreme it probably profaned its own values, and led not infrequently to adultery. Courtly Love, with its new concept of romantic love of men for women added fresh heights of pleasure and abysses of grief to the lives of noble ladies, but beyond the highest ranks of society it would not have affected the generally accepted view that women were inferior beings.

The troubadours, born vassals of Eleanor of Aquitaine, inevitably made her the object of poetic veneration. To her influence, both directly as the patroness of poets and indirectly as the mistress of Henry Plantagenet's vast domains, is partly credited the spread of Courtly Love from southern to northern Europe, where, in the later twelfth century the *trouvères* of northern France and the *minnesinger* of Germany celebrated their ladies and composed romances with all the zest of their southern counterparts.

Eleanor's patronage of Courtly Love was not wholeheartedly encouraged by either of her husbands; as Louis VII had ordered Marcabru from his court, Henry II did likewise with one of the greatest of troubadours, Bernard of Ventadour. Casual infidelity was a pleasure in which Henry indulged, but he had no intention of permitting the impression to arise that the same privilege extended to his queen.

But, though troubadours were sometimes unwelcome to kings and lords as potential seducers of their wives, they could not be condemned on the one hand as unworldly romantics and on the other as non-combatant womanizers. Some of them came from the ranks of the nobility, and sang of war as well as love. Bertran de Born, troubadour and lord of Hautfort, loved war more than women: here follows one of his verses, in the original *langue d'oc*, and in translation:

Bela m'es pressa de blezos,
Cobertz de teintz vermelhs e blaus,
D'entresenhs e de gonfanos
De diversas colors tretaus,
Tendas et traps e rics pavilhos tendre
Lanzas frassar, escutz trancar e fendre
Elmes brunitz, e colps donar e prendre
(I love the medley of blazons
Enamelled scarlet, gold and blue,
The standards and the gonfalons
Painted in every vivid hue;
I love the tents that decorate the field,
I love to break a lance, or pierce a shield,
Or cleave a helm and call on foes to yield.)

These words serve as a reminder that everywhere throughout Henry's dominions men were thinking such thoughts, even if few could express them so well. Henry's ceaseless travels were far from being royal tours in the twentieth-century sense of the word. They were in part administrative and judicial tours of duty, in part military expeditions. After Aquitaine had received a visitation in 1156, Wales was the scene of a campaign in 1157.

Peter of Blois wrote in praise of Henry 'Above everything in the world that one may desire or work after, he labours for peace; all that he thinks, all that he says, all that he does is directed to this end: that his people may have tranquil days.' But one may say without satire that Henry was always fighting somebody in the interests of keeping everybody at peace.

Historians have given the title of 'Angevin Empire' to the patchwork of kingdom, duchies and lordships which Henry had acquired through conquest, inheritance and marriage. The resulting agglomeration lacked naturally defensible frontiers.

Henry was always seeking to secure his boundaries, and to him the best method of so doing appeared to be by extending them to geographically advantageous limits. The map on page 44 shows Henry's 'empire', and the lands of which he hoped to acquire possession or suzerainty: these were the

The Angevin Empire
Aberdeen
Edinburgh
Carlisle
Durham
Armargh
York
Dublin
Chester
Cork
Bristol
London
Southampton
BRABANT
FLANDERS
HAINAULT
VERMANDOIS
EU
Rouen
VEXIN
Caen
Lisieux
Chateau Gaillard
NORMANDY
Paris
CHAMPAGNE
Mortain
BLOIS
Seine
BRITTANY
MAINE
Le Mans
Blois
Loire
ANJOU
Angers
Tours
Nantes
TOURAINE
Chinon
BURGUNDY
Fontevrault
BERRI
POITOU
Poitiers
Chateauroux
La Rochelle
Lusignan
LA MARCHE
SAINTONGE
ANGOUMOIS
Limoges
Angoulême
LIMOUSIN
AUVERGNE
Perigueux
PERIGORD
Dordogne
Bordeaux
AGENAIS
Agen
Garonne
Montauban
TOULOUSE
GASCONY
Toulouse
PROVENCE
Lands inherited by Henry II, or acquired by conquest resulting from hereditary claim
Lands permanently or temporarily acknowledging suzerainty of Henry II or his successors
Lands acquired by Henry II on his marriage to Eleanor of Aquitaine
Lands of the Royal House of France

duchy of Brittany, the area called the Norman Vexin, and the county of Toulouse.

Brittany fell conveniently under Henry's influence through an unexpected chain of circumstances. In 1148 Conan III, Duke of Brittany, died leaving rival claimants to the duchy; but, in 1156, the city of Nantes rejected both aspirants and offered itself with all of lower Brittany to Henry's younger brother, Geoffrey. This arrangement was acceptable to both of them, since Henry had unjustly withheld from his brother the lands which their father had intended Geoffrey should inherit. The offer of lower Brittany to Geoffrey removed this cause of contention between them.

Geoffrey's sudden death in 1158 enabled Henry, as his heir, to claim lower Brittany. Though he had not gained complete possession of Brittany, he had made a great advance towards it, and Louis VII acknowledged the reality of the situation by recognizing Henry's claim to the honorific title of 'Seneschal of Brittany'.

The Vexin was disputed territory between Normandy and the Ile de France. Count Geoffrey Plantagenet had ceded the castle of Gisors, which commanded the Vexin, to Louis VII as the price of Louis' recognition of his right to rule Normandy, and Henry had ceded the whole of the Vexin to Louis when he did homage for Normandy in 1152. But Henry regarded this agreement as temporary, and by 1158 he had thought of a method of recovering the loss.

Louis VII, after the annulment of his marriage to Eleanor, had married Constance of Castile, who bore him a daughter named Margaret. Henry proposed a marriage between Margaret and his own son Henry, who was his heir, since William, his eldest son by Eleanor, had died in 1156. He suggested that the Vexin should be Margaret's dowry.

The preliminary negotiations were carried out by Thomas Becket, who entered Paris in June 1158, at the head of an embassy of unrivalled splendour. The French had never seen a king – certainly not their own austere Louis – travel with so opulent a household as the King of England's chancellor. Preceding him walked a procession of 250 squires and pages, a host of falconers bearing their hooded birds, a multitude of kennel boys leading couples of hounds; then followed a long train of decorated wagons, each drawn by five horses and preceded by a groom leading a great mastiff. The wagons were followed by twelve pack mules, each one led by a servant wearing the King of England's livery, and ridden by a tame monkey! Last of all, escorted by knights and men-at-arms, came Thomas Becket, mounted on a great destrier – a knight's warhorse. A mule was considered the proper mount for a cleric; but Becket was scarcely a conventional cleric.

Becket's diplomatic skill was not inferior to his flair for organizing a spectacle; he secured Louis' agreements to the marriage of Margaret and young Henry. The terms were concluded at a meeting between the two kings themselves in August 1158: Margaret was to be brought up in England, and the three main strongholds of the Vexin–Gisors, Neufle and Neufmarché–were to be placed in the custody of three Knights Templar until the royal children were of an age to marry, when the Vexin would pass into Angevin possession.

The Templars were considered suitable guardians as they were members of an international chivalric order, subject to neither king. However, their custodianship of the three castles was brief, for the transfer of the Vexin took place in 1160, far sooner than Louis might reasonably have expected. Without his consent, Henry had the marriage of the two small children solemnized and then claimed the Vexin strongholds. He thus acquired the coveted territory by an adroit if scarcely honest manipulation of the terms of his agreement with Louis.

He was less successful in his endeavour to win control of Toulouse, which he attempted in 1159. Eleanor's ancestors had at one time been acknowledged suzerains of the counts of Toulouse, and Henry was eager to press his claim to suzerainty in right of his wife, with the ulterior motive of extending the boundaries of Angevin influence to the Mediterranean coast.

However, Raymond V, Count of Toulouse, was married to Louis VII's sister, and he acknowledged the King of France as his suzerain. He appealed to Louis for help in resisting what he regarded as Angevin aggression, and not a lawful claim upon his homage.

In June 1159 Henry marched on the city of Toulouse with a great army which included a contingent brought by his kinsman Malcolm IV, King of Scots, and a host of seven hundred knights equipped by Thomas Becket. On this expedition Becket acquitted himself more like a knight than a cleric; his personal exploits included the defeat of a French champion of some renown, Engelram de Trie.

But Henry was doomed to discomfiture, Louis responded to Count Raymond's appeal, and came in person to occupy Toulouse. Henry was prepared to attempt to overawe Raymond, and to skirmish with French troops, but he would not attack a city occupied by the king whose vassal he was for his continental domains. To do so would set a bad example to his own vassals. He withdrew. Louis had outfaced him by a means which was characteristically correct. It was a small setback for Henry, but it rankled; possibly Henry's dishonest acquisition of the Vexin the following year contained an element of revenge.

By 1160, apart from the Toulouse question, there was little to ruffle Henry's complacency. He could look back over a decade which had seen him progress triumphantly from nascent ambition to the mastery of an empire. Eleanor had borne him four sons, of whom three – Henry, Richard and Geoffrey – lived and thrived, and his family was still growing. All in all, he had much to thank God for, and no doubt he did so in the confident conviction that God was on his side.

Woodcarving depicting the Coronation of the Virgin. To the men of the twelfth century the inferiority of women was an unquestioned fact of life. But there was one exception: the Blessed Virgin Mary presented the greatest example of perfected humanity after Christ Himself (J. C. D. SMITH)

Troubadours and the Cult of Courtly Love

William 'The Good', King of Sicily, offers the Church of Monreale to the Blessed Virgin Mary. The increasing cult of the Blessed Virgin is thought by some scholars to have given rise to the Cult of Courtly Love, by introducing the possibility of an element of adoration for womanhood into secular love. An alternative, or parallel, influence has been seen in the poetry of Islamic Spain, where women enjoyed greater respect than in northern Europe during the early Middle Ages (SCALA)

An ivory relief-carving showing (above) *the Virgin Mary as Queen of Heaven, holding the infant Jesus and* (below) *a tournament scene, showing at each side knights kneeling at the feet of their ladies. Whether the quasi-religious element in the Cult of Courtly Love was ennobling or blasphemous doubtless varied with the characters of the lovers in each individual relationship* (MANSELL COLLECTION)

Knights jousting, watched by their ladies (PICTUREPOINT)

A knight rescues a lady from a wild man. Chivalrous treatment of women, an ideal of knightly conduct, was encouraged by the Cult of Courtly Love (PICTUREPOINT)

Courtly Love, rejecting the brutal materialism of the feudal marriage market, led to civilized sharing of leisure between men and women. (Above) *young lovers play chess,* (below) *they play merelles, or 'Nine Men's Morris'* (RADIO TIMES HULTON PICTURE LIBRARY)

An enamelled casket, believed to depict scenes from the story of Tristram and Yseult (or Tristan and Isolde), one of the great romances of Courtly Love (BRITISH MUSEUM)

A troubadour, received in the bedchamber of a queen, sings to her accompanied by a musician. Not all kings encouraged the entertainment of troubadours by their queens; the troubadour Marcabru was banished from the French Court, and Bernard of Ventadour from the Court of England (ARCHIV FÜR KUNST UND GESCHICHTE)

(left) *An idyllic scene, showing the* minnesinger (*or German equivalent of the southern troubadour*) *Bruno von Hornberg, with his lady* (UNIVERSITY LIBRARY, HEIDELBERG)

(right) *Courtly Love was not always as sublimated as its inspiration presupposed. A* minnesinger *is ingeniously drawn up to his lady's chamber, not perhaps for any innocent purpose* (UNIVERSITY LIBRARY, HEIDELBERG)

(below) *A man and woman, represented as two doves. Doves were traditionally sacred to Venus, and so this charming carving is probably intended to be an allegory of lust, and a castigation of the betrayal of Courtly Love* (J. C. D. SMITH)

III
King and Saint

Becket *One thing is simple.*
Whoever is made Archbishop will very soon
Offend either you, Henry, or his God . . .
As Chancellor my whole mind could speak for yours,
Because I knew the Church had for her tongue
A scholar and a saintly man who was not to be
Browbeaten. But now Theobald is dead.
The English Church has lost its tongue. Do you mean
That I should now become that tongue,
To be used in argument between you and me?
Because, if so, we shall not be as we have been.

(Christopher Fry, *Curtmantle*, Act I)

Archbishop Theobald of Canterbury died in April 1161. King Henry had already decided who should be his successor, but when he broached his idea, Thomas Becket cast a self-deprecating glance at his rich clothes and exclaimed, 'How religious and saintly is the man you want to appoint to that holy see!'

No doubt Henry laughed in response. Of course Thomas Becket was not saintly, but Henry did not want a saintly archbishop; he wanted a man who would combine the offices of Chancellor of England and Archbishop of Canterbury, and continue to be his right-hand man, keeping Church and State running smoothly in harness under his authority. The outcome was the absolute reversal of his intentions.

Thomas Becket knew himself better than Henry knew him. He was a perfectionist; whatever he did, he did to the uttermost of his power. As chancellor he had striven to be the mirror of his master's greater glory. That was what he conceived a chancellor's duty to be. He conceived it the duty of an archbishop to be a religious and saintly man, a servant of God and a shepherd of souls. Becket warned Henry that the offices of chancellor and archbishop might well represent conflicting interests; but intelligent foresight is not prophecy, and though Becket could foresee probable conflict he could not prophesy certain incompatibility.

Henry saw the situation differently. He saw Becket as his friend and collaborator for seven years; a man who owed him much, and would owe him more. Becket had not scrupled to extract money from the Church on grounds of dubious legality for the war against Toulouse; Henry had no reason to suppose that Becket would refuse to serve his interests in a similar manner in future. Henry has been accused of poor judgment in securing Becket's appointment as archbishop; Becket has been accused of disingenuous ambition for accepting it. But what man can see his own way forward when it leads round a sharp corner?

Becket was ordained priest on 2 June 1162, and the following day he was consecrated archbishop by Henry of Winchester. The experience transformed him, as in the light of his self-knowledge he had probably feared that it might. He resolved the impossibility of co-existing with his former self by sending the king his resignation from the chancellorship.

Henry was confounded. The conflict in Becket's inner life had no meaning for him; all he saw was an act which from the outside looked like a treacherous *volte face*.

The king had had concrete reasons for desiring to see his chancellor at the head of the Church in England. He had hoped by this means to find a workable solution to a growing problem which bedevilled the administration of justice. The problem had been summed up succinctly by Henry's most recent biographer.

> There were in England two separate systems of jurisdiction, covering the entire country: the royal courts and the ecclesiastical courts. The latter were responsible for all men in holy orders and other matters ranging from Church property to marriage contracts, oaths and wills. If a man who was no more than a deacon or clerk committed an offence, it was to this court that he had to answer. Henry's complaint was not against the competence of the Church courts, but their lack of punitive powers. A layman committing murder would be heavily fined, mutilated or imprisoned; a cleric guilty of the same offence would be deprived of his orders and go scot-free, defrocking being the greatest punishment that the ecclesiastical court could impose.

It has been reckoned that in Henry's England one man in thirty was a cleric, which gives some idea of the scale of the problem. The contemporary statement that since the beginning of Henry's reign one hundred murders had been committed by clerics illustrates the scale of the resultant injustice. Many a shrewd ruffian must have sought minor orders to insure his life should his crimes catch up with him. The Church was much to blame for not examining the quality of its lowest grade of recruits.

In the interests of justice and order Henry had to find a solution to this problem, and he had looked to Becket to assist him in adjusting the conflicting claims of the two jurisdictions. But the new-fledged primate disappointed his hopes. Becket, who had been no more clerical in spirit than some of those who had found themselves arraigned before the Church courts, newly identifying himself as a churchman, took up the most extreme defence of the Church courts which the interpretation of canon law would allow.

When Henry returned from a prolonged visit to Normandy in January 1163 he had a cordial meeting with Becket, and with his eldest son Prince Henry, who was being educated in Becket's household. But thenceforward a series of clashes over disputes involving canon law eroded their friendship and brought them to the threshold of enmity.

Becket excommunicated one William of Eynsford, who was a tenant-in-chief of the king, without first warning Henry, a course of action which was contrary to custom since a tenant-in-chief might well hold office of state, and excommunication, since it was intended to sever a man from the Christian community, would inhibit him in the performance of his official duties. Becket further offended the king by forbidding the marriage of his youngest brother William to Isabella de Warenne, the widow of King Stephen's bastard son. The intended marriage was believed to have been that rare phenomenon of the twelfth century, a love match, and William's sudden death was generally imputed to a broken heart. But, from the present-day viewpoint least excusably, Becket defended from punishment by a lay court a cleric found guilty before a Church court of rape and murder.

Becket took his stand upon a quotation from St Jerome's commentary on the prophet Nahum: *Nec enim Deus judicat bis in idipsum* ('God judges no man twice in the same matter'). Henry did not take up an extreme position against this view; he did not demand a second trial. He agreed that an acquittal before an ecclesiastical court should be accepted; but he demanded that if a 'criminous clerk' (a cleric who had committed a crime) were found guilty by a Church court, he should be handed over to the secular authorities to suffer the same punishment as a layman for his crime.

The matter was argued before a council held at Westminster in October 1163, where the king urged that his view of the rights and wrongs of the dispute was supported by the ancient customs of the kingdom. He requested the bishops to swear to observe these customs; but, sensing a threat to the independence of the Church, with one exception they followed Becket in agreeing to take the required oath only if it contained the ambigiuous clause 'saving our order'.

Becket and Henry were now openly at enmity, but Becket's position was not a strong one. If he were to press his arguments to the utmost limits he required full papal support; but the present pope, Alexander III, was unable to accord the backing which would have given him victory. The death in

1159 of Pope Adrian IV (who was Nicholas Breakspear, the only Englishman ever to be pope) had been followed by a disputed election, after which Pope Alexander III had suffered from the disadvantageous existence of a rival 'Anti-Pope' who enjoyed the support of the Holy Roman Emperor, Frederick Barbarossa. However much Alexander III might have sympathized with Becket, he had to adapt his attitudes to the exigencies of political pressure.

At first the pope was more embarrassed than grateful for Becket's championship, and he sent the Abbot of l'Aumône to Becket, advising him to yield to the king's demands. At Oxford, in December 1163, Becket promised to observe what Henry claimed to be the 'ancient customs' of the realm.

Though Becket was not a man made for compromises, his obedience to the pope might have been made to appear as a compromise had Henry chosen to accept it in that spirit. But, since he was as uncompromising as Becket, he proceeded to the definition of the ancient customs, in a famous document 'The Constitutions of Clarendon'.

At Clarendon, which was Henry's favourite palace and hunting lodge, near Salisbury, the King's council met to study and to swear to observe the customs which Henry declared had been followed during the reigns of his Norman ancestors.

Of the sixteen clauses of the document not all were controversial. Some concerned the rights enjoyed and the duties owed by churchmen within the feudal structure. But those which aroused the hostility of Becket, and the English bishops who steadfastly supported him, concerned the right of the clergy to excommunicate tenants-in-chief, the right of the clergy to leave the kingdom without the permission of the king, the right of appeal from ecclesiastical courts in England to the papal court, and most serious of all, the right of ecclesiastical courts to judge criminous clerks. The king's attempt to forbid these clerical privileges, on the ground that his ancestors had successfully done so, at first met with stiff opposition until, to the astonishment of his bishops, Becket suddenly gave way, and advised the rest to follow.

He was much condemned, both then and later, for having capitulated; especially as it appeared that he had done so as a result of threats of physical violence offered by the king's more ardent supporters. Possibly he lost his nerve in the face of these threats because, although he had the backing of the English bishops, he felt his position insecure since he lacked the ultimate support of the pope. But, shortly after his undignified surrender, he began to suffer agonies of remorse. He inflicted extravagant penances upon himself, and made two unsuccessful attempts to flee the country to seek papal absolution for his 'perjury'.

The unexpected result of Henry's codification of the 'customs', and of the compulsion which he put upon Becket, was to drive the pope into unequivocal support of Becket's initial resistance.

When Alexander III saw a copy of 'The Constitutions of Clarendon', which, since they affected the Church, Henry was obliged to send him, he was appalled by the limitations which Henry was seeking to impose upon the powers of the Church; naturally he could not be expected to take into consideration Henry's practical concern for the rationalization of judicial practice in his kingdom. His reaction was forthright condemnation of the majority of Henry's provisions, and clear support for Becket.

Thereafter Henry's struggle with Becket ceased to be an honest if unnecessary confrontation of principles, and became a bitter personal quarrel. Here Henry was at fault in initiating a campaign of merciless and unjust harassment, culminating at the Council of Northampton in October 1164.

Becket was summond to Northampton to answer the appeal of one John the Marshal who had a case relating to an estate in Sussex decided against him in the archbishop's court. When the appeal had been previously arranged to take place at Westminster, Becket had pleaded sickness and had not attended. In view of his later conduct his excuse was probably a true one, and Henry's response to it part of an attempt to ruin him.

When Becket appeared at Northampton he found himself condemned unheard for contempt of court, which was Henry's chosen interpretation of his non-appearance at Westminster, and sentenced to pay a heavy fine. Henry went on to demand accounts for all the sums of money which had been spent by Becket during his chancellorship, and for vast sums which were supposed to have accrued to him.

Becket's answer was the he had come to Northampton only to answer the appeal of John the Marshal, that he could not produce his accounts at such short notice, that all the money which had passed through his hands had been spent in the king's service, and finally that when he had been appointed archbishop he had been formally released from his liabilities incurred as chancellor. This was true, for his pupil Prince Henry had released him at the request of Bishop Henry of Winchester; a perfectly correct move at the time, but one which weakened the King's case against Becket.

At the final session of the Council of Northampton Becket appeared carrying the metropolitan cross of the see of Canterbury in his own hands, instead of having it carried before him. It was a symbolic act intended to illustrate that he saw the Church persecuted in his own person, and that he would carry the cross of persecution if necessary to the point of martyrdom.

Robert, Earl of Leicester, the justiciar, was commanded by Henry to pronounce sentence upon Becket for the offences alleged against him; but Becket, with the awesome authority of his office, forbade the justiciar to speak, and strode from the hall still carrying his cross.

He departed from Northampton unscathed, and a few days later successfully fled the country. He made his way to the papal court, which was at Sens, as the Anti-Pope was in occupation of Rome. Becket offered his episcopal ring to Alexander III with the words: 'These evils have come upon the English Church through my fault. I climbed up into the sheepfold of Christ, I entered not by the strait gate of canonical election. I was thrust in by worldly influence. I was reluctant to accept office, it is true, but nothing can change the fact that my election was the work of men. It was not God's work. Is it to be wondered at if it has ended in disaster?'

And, in the uninhibited manner of the age, he wept openly.

The pope was deeply moved. He returned Becket's ring, and though opinion among his cardinals was divided as to whether he should or should not accept Becket's abdication, he declared: 'It is right that this man should be restored to office, whether he wants it or not. He has been fighting our battles and he is entitled to our wholehearted support.'

If Becket's cause was controversial at the papal court, it was far more so in England. Becket's tergiversations had divided the English bishops against him. He had two personal enemies among them: one was Roger of Pont-l'Evêque, Archbishop of York, whose dislike of Becket dated from the days when they had both been protégés of Theobald of Canterbury, but who, on his elevation to the see of York, had inherited the northern archieposcopate's resentment of the primacy of Canterbury; the other was Gilbert Foliot, formerly Bishop of Hereford, and since 1163 Bishop of London, whose long and distinguished career as a Cistercian monk and a blameless prelate may have led him to expect election to the archbishopric of Canterbury himself. He could not have failed to regard Becket, whose ordination antedated his consecration as archbishop by twenty-four hours, as a parvenu. His disapproval of Becket's extravagant championship of the judicial rights of the Church may well have been justified, but his enmity could not fail to suggest the flavour of sour grapes. Of Becket's dramatic behaviour at Northampton Foliot remarked '*Semper fuit stultus et semper erit*' ('He was always a fool and he always will be'). However, the fact that respected English prelates failed to support Becket strengthened King Henry's position once again.

The conflict of Becket and Henry became an international *cause célèbre*. In 1165 Henry considered playing his trump card, and transferring his spiritual allegiance to the Anti-Pope Paschal III. Since Henry was the ally of the Emperor Frederick Barbarossa he could have done so with political advantage. But Henry, whatever his personal failings and his secular pragmatism, was *au fond* a faithful son of the Church. He might quarrel with his primate, but in the last resort it would have outraged his conscience to repudiate the lawfully elected pope.

From 1164 to 1170 Thomas Becket remained in exile, for the most part a resident of the Cistercian abbey at Pontigny. There he subjected himself physically to the austere monastic discipline, while he continued with increasing vigour to fight his religio-political battles by correspondence.

King Louis VII, who was already the protector of the pope, delighted to become the protector of Becket, so long as the latter remained at enmity with his king. Yet at the same time Louis saw his duty in seeking to reconcile king and primate, if a reasonable accommodation of political and spiritual interests could be achieved. Between 1165 and 1170 he negotiated twelve interviews with Henry, ten of which took place. On these occasions, according to a leading historian of the period, 'reconcillation of the King and the Archbishop was if not the only, at least a prominent subject of discussion'.

Becket and Henry were brought face to face at Montmirail in Maine on 6 January 1169, and in the autumn of the same year at Montmartre, which was then a hill outside Paris. But for all the good offices of Louis VII reconciliation was impossible: Becket would agree to anything, so long as he was permitted to agree 'saving the honour of God' or 'saving his order'; Henry would show an uncharacteristic spirit of compromise, yet he would not give Becket the 'kiss of peace', the symbolic embrace which signified good faith. No amount of negotiation could remove the mutual suspicion of the adversaries, or restore the trust which had once lain at the foundations of their friendship.

The long struggle might have been ended more tamely and more swiftly than it was, had the pope felt free to ignore political pressures; but the papal legates appointed to attempt to break the deadlock were subject to the same limitations as the pope himself. Becket's cause demanded the support of the Church; the Papacy could not risk losing the support of Henry.

In 1170 Henry began to take thought for the succession, and he sought permission of the pope to have Prince Henry crowned. The coronation of the heir during the father's lifetime was a practice known in France, but in the absence of a clear rule of primogeniture, not previously introduced into England. Pope Alexander III thought it politic to agree to the coronation of Henry the younger.

The privilege of crowning the kings of England belonged to the Archbishop of Canterbury, but since the exiled Becket could not crown the young king, it was done by the Archbishop of York, with six assisting bishops in attendance.

The outrage offered to Canterbury and to Becket personally added new virulence to the six-year-old quarrel. The pope had seen the danger, changed his mind at the last moment, and written forbidding the king to have his son crowned by the Archbishop of York, but the letters had not arrived until after the ceremony had taken place. King Louis was offended because his daughter Margaret, the young king's wife, had not been crowned with her husband. With Becket, the pope and Louis ranged against him, Henry agreed to negotiate once more.

For the last time Henry and Becket met at Fréteval and went through a form of reconciliation, with no word about the Constitutions of Clarendon, and no kiss of peace. The hollowness of the proceedings must have been apparent to all present, but Becket was free at last to return to Canterbury.

Thomas Becket crossed the Channel with the pope's permission to take punitive action against the bishops who had participated in young Henry's coronation. On his arrival in England he suspended the Archbishop of York and the bishops of London and Salisbury from their priestly functions; and in the case of Gilbert Foliot, he allowed himself the additional satisfaction of excommunicating him. All three of them immediately went to Normandy, where Henry had remained, to complain of Becket's treatment of them.

In the resultant explosion of Angevin fury with which Henry received the report, he was heard to utter the famous, fatal words, 'Will nobody rid me of this turbulent priest?' There were present four knights of the king's household – Reginald Fitzurse, William de Tracy, Hugh de Moreville and Reginald le Breton – who took the king's outburst as a command, and set off for England immediately, to carry it out.

To Henry's credit it should be remembered that as soon as his temper had cooled, and the departure of the four knights had been noticed, he sent a messenger spurring after them, to prevent their all too obvious purpose. But the messenger never caught up with them.

On 29 December 1170 the four knights reached Canterbury, and murdered the archbishop in a side chapel of the cathedral. He died facing them with the courage of a knight, and unresisting in the spirit of a martyr.

The news was brought to Henry on 1 January 1171, and he received it with the horror of a man who recognized his ultimate responsibility, even if not his direct guilt. Between Henry and Becket the clash of personalities had been as violent as a mortal combat between two armed knights. The issue itself was blurred by the drama of the conclusion.

On 21 February 1173 Pope Alexander III canonized Thomas Becket, both in response to the spontaneous cult of the martyred archbishop and in recognition of his services to the Church. That St Thomas had indulged in excessive fasting and self-flagellation and had worn a hair shirt infested with lice impressed the popular mind of the twelfth century as evidences of his sanctity. His holiness and heroism made him the object of ardent devotion. He became the 'holy, blissful martyr' whose shrine was the destination of Chaucer's Canterbury Pilgrims; until the Reformation, he surpassed St Edward the Confessor and preceded St George in popular esteem as the patron of England.

The pope, who had known Thomas Becket as human and fallible, intransigent and indomitable, may have observed the growing cult with detached scepticism. The Church has always found it difficult to accommodate its saints while they live. Thomas Becket alive had been at times a political liability; St Thomas dead left Henry Plantagenet vulnerable to all his enemies.

Religion and the Power of the Church

Religion dominated the lives of twelfth-century men and women: the power of God, the hope of heaven and the fear of hell, were never far from their thoughts

(above) *The origin of all things: God the Father, represented as the architect of the Universe* (OSTERREICHES NATIONALBIBLIOTHEK, VIENNA)

(below left) *Christ enthroned in majesty, as the judge of mankind, from a carving by one of the greatest sculptors of the middle ages, Gislebertus of Autun* (STUDIO E. M. JANET LE CAISNE)

(below right) *The judgment of the dead. Angels and devils weigh the souls of the dead: the blessed ascend to heaven, and the damned are cast down into hell. The carving is part of the relief by Gislebertus, from the tympanum of Autun Cathedral* (STUDIO E. M. JANET LE CAISNE)

Human and benign is the image of Our Lady and her Son, drawn by Matthew Paris. Love of Christ as the merciful redeemer and of His mother as the unfailing intercessor for sinners, began to take the place of the crude fear of hell in the spiritual life of the aspirant for heaven (BRITISH MUSEUM)

The inexorability of the judgment could be mitigated by kindly intercessors. A female saint, possibly Our Lady herself, intervenes to save a soul, while a devil attempts to cheat by tipping the scales (PICTUREPOINT)

The influence of the Church upon a religion-orientated society would be hard to exaggerate. The power of the Church was awesomely expressed by its rich and splendid buildings. Nowadays cathedrals and churches are almost dwarfed by higher modern buildings; in the twelfth century they towered triumphantly above substantial merchants' houses, crowded hovels and city walls alike. The church of Notre Dame La Grande in Eleanor of Aquitaine's capital city of Poitiers, a superb example of the church architecture of the age (H. ROGER-VIOLLET)

The sanctuary knocker of Durham Cathedral, the symbol of the privilege of sanctuary which the Church extended to the fugitive. Sanctuary offered a literally heaven-sent means of escape for a victim of injustice, but its misuse could lead to the flouting of law and order, if the privilege of sanctuary were claimed by a criminal (MANSELL COLLECTION)

The Papal Court. The Popes, as 'Vicars of Christ' claimed authority over secular rulers: the reality of the claim fluctuated with political conditions (RADIO TIMES HULTON PICTURE LIBRARY)

Innocent III, one of the most powerful Popes of the Middle Ages. During his tenure of the papacy (1198–1216), England became a fief of the Holy See, though King John's motives for accepting this state of affairs were not wholeheartedly dutiful (MANSELL COLLECTION)

A bishop writing. The Church could be the way of advancement for men of humble origins, like Thomas Becket. Literacy was not the absolute monopoly of the clergy, but it would be near the truth to say that scholarship was. Scholars who contributed to the intellectual movement known as the 'Twelfth Century Renaissance' – Adelard of Bath, Peter Abelard, St Bernard of Clairvaux, John of Salisbury, and many others – had nothing in common except Holy Orders (BRITISH MUSEUM)

Vignettes illustrating the monastic ideal of withdrawal from the world into a life of prayer and contemplation (BRITISH MUSEUM)

Contact between the Church and the laity: monks preaching to shepherds (BRITISH MUSEUM)

A reliquary of St Thomas Becket, decorated with a representation of his martyrdom. Belief in the efficacy of holy relics to perform miraculous cures led many people to make pilgrimages to churches which possessed the relics of saints (MANSELL COLLECTION)

A selection of medieval pilgrims' badges. Pilgrimages were considered meritorious acts of devotion in themselves, and pilgrims purchased badges at the shrines which they visited (RADIO TIMES HULTON PICTURE LIBRARY)

A humorously irreverent representation of a less serious sinner: a monastic cellarer giving way to self-indulgence (RADIO TIMES HULTON PICTURE LIBRARY)

Despite its power and prestige, the medieval church had its feet of clay in its unworthy members. At worst there were the 'criminous clerks' (ie clerics who committed crimes) whose punishment became a matter of controversy in the reign of Henry II. A monk and a nun undergo punishment in the stocks (BRITISH LIBRARY)

IV
The Devil's Descendants

Henry *Dear Christ, the day that any man would dread*
Is when life goes separate from the man,
When he speaks what he doesn't say, and does
What is not his doing, and an hour of the day
Which was unimportant as it went by
Comes back revealed as the satan of all hours,
Which will never let the man go. And then
He would see how the natural poisons in him
Creep from everything he sees and touches
As though saying, 'Here is the world you created
In your own image.' But this is not the world
He would have made. Sprung from a fraction of life,
A hair-fine crack in the dam, the unattended
Moment sweeps away the whole attempt,
The heart, thoughts, belief, longing
And intention of the man. It is infamous,
This life is infamous, if it uses us
Against our knowledge or will.

(Christopher Fry, *Curtmantle*, Act II)

One day a baron named Ralph de Albini threw a stone at Henry II, an act for which he forfeited the manor of Didcot. It was a light punishment for a gross insult to the king's person. Henry was not unduly perturbed by acts of enmity; he had had powerful enemies since before he had emerged from boyhood. However, he could not ignore or shrug off the universal enmity with which he was regarded after the murder of Thomas Becket. His quarrel with Becket and its aftermath probably prevented him from seeing what was happening under his very nose: he was so beset by enemies that he did not notice the animosity against him which was growing within the circle of his own family.

Eleanor of Aquitaine bore Henry a total of eight children, seven of whom reached adulthood. The eldest, William, it may be remembered, had died in early childhood. Henry (who after his coronation was generally known as 'the Young King') was born in 1155; the first daughter, Matilda, who became Duchess of Saxony, was born the following year. In 1157 the future King Richard I was born, followed by Geoffrey in 1159. Eleanor, who became Queen of Castile, was born in 1161, and Joanna, who became Queen of Sicily, in 1165. John, the last born, entered the world on Christmas Eve 1167. His mother was then forty-five years old.

After John's birth the relationship of Henry and Eleanor deteriorated rapidly. In earlier years Eleanor had ignored Henry's frequent but extremely casual infidelities, which had occurred in the course of his ceaseless journeyings, whenever his mood was amorous, and whenever a pretty, willing girl had caught his eye. But in the mid-1160s, when Henry was still in his prime and Eleanor was undeniably middle-aged, Henry fell deeply in love for perhaps the only time in his life. His liaison with Rosamond de Çlifford, the legendary 'Fair Rosamond', was at first kept secret, but it was not long a secret from Eleanor. Her reaction can be summed up by the well known words:

> Heav'n has no rage, like love to hatred turn'd
> Nor Hell a fury, like a woman scorn'd.

Henry and Eleanor both desired the greater glory of their children, but their competition for their children's affection added its inevitably baneful influence to marital strife. The girls were not at the heart of the problem. The advantageous marriages arranged for them enhanced Angevin influence and gratified parental ambitions. But the problem of making provision for the boys converted bitterness into actual warfare, and the reaction of the Plantagenet princes to their father's efforts on their behalf made the family legend of satanic descent begin to appear convincing.

The three elder boys were closer to their mother than their father, while John was his father's favourite. This situation created a fertile soil for the seeds of trouble to grow in, and the four princes, with their diverse imperfections, nourished those seeds and produced a rank harvest.

Henry 'the Young King' had received his early education in the household of Thomas Becket, then the worldly and flamboyant chancellor. His father's quarrel with Becket led to his removal from this environment, so that he had not been subjected to the austere, disciplinary influence of Becket's later years. He respected Becket's memory, while remaining the mirror of his worldly period.

The next influence upon the young Henry was his military tutor, William Marshal. William was the fourth son of a minor Wiltshire baron, a landless youth who became the hero of an age, and was to die as Regent of England. He earned his early living by his prowess in tournaments, the mock battles in which knights kept themselves in training for real warfare, and could win rich prizes by ransoming their defeated opponents and capturing their destriers – for the warhorse was the knight's most valued possession.

The following incident, related in a biographical epic poem *L'Historie de Guillaume le Maréchal*, will illustrate the aspect of chivalric life which influenced the Young King. William Marshal rode to Joigny to attend a tournament, and Aelis, Countess of Joigny, came with her ladies to witness the day's deeds. Someone suggested that while the arrival of the opposing knights was awaited, those already present should dance. William Marshal composed a song to accompany the dancing. Then a young herald took his place, and while William and the ladies danced he sang a song with the refrain 'Marshal, I need a good horse.' Suddenly the opposing knights arrived, and without a word William Marshal dropped out of the dance, vaulted on to his destrier, challenged one of the new arrivals, immediately unhorsed him, and leading the captured destrier back to his companions, presented it to the herald, who continued singing, altering his refrain to 'I have a horse, the Marshal gave it me.'

William Marshal was not only the object of admiration for his knightly prowess, he was renowned throughout Christendom for his personal integrity. The Young King admired him for the former, yet seemed impervious to the influence of the latter.

The pupil of Becket and William Marshal was described by a contemporary as 'a prodigy of unfaith, a lovely palace of sin', for he imitated the glamorous qualities of his mentors, but not the sterner aspect of their natures. It was easier for him to plot a smooth course through the world by employing his beauty, charm, wit and generosity to win friends and to influence people. It was not surprising that though Henry II had his eldest son crowned as his lawful successor he refused to let him enjoy more than the outward show of kingship; yet also it was not surprising that the Young King resented the fact that his coronation had made him a king only in name, and thirsted to enjoy the reality of power.

Richard, of all the Plantagenet princes, was closest to his mother. While young Henry, as the eldest son, was to inherit England, Normandy, Anjou and Maine, it was agreed by Henry and Eleanor that Richard should be his mother's heir, and inherit Aquitaine and Poitou.

After the estrangement of his parents Richard spent his time with his mother at Poitiers, where Eleanor began to reassert herself as the native ruler of her subjects, with the ultimate intention that Richard should assume the position of her knightly protector and guardian of her possessions. Disappointed in turn by two husbands, Eleanor began to look for emotional fulfilment in the love of her favourite son.

At the same time Eleanor could enjoy once again her role as the patroness of poets. She was still the toast of northern Europe. German students sang:

Waer diu werlt alliu min
von dem mere unz an den Rin,
des wolt ih mih darben,
daz diu künegin von Engellant
laege an minen armen.
(If all the world were mine
From the seashore to the Rhine,
All I'd give away,
If the Queen of England
In my arms lay.)

And Bernard of Ventadour, once more a welcomed admirer, could write:

Domna, vostre sui e serai,
Del vostre servizi garnitz.
Vostr' om sui juratz e plevitz,
E vostre m'era des abans.
E vos etz lo meus jois primers,
E si seretz vos los derrers,
Tan com la vida m'er durañs.
(Lady, I'm yours and yours shall be,
Vowed to your service constantly,
This is the oath of fealty
I pledged to you this long time past.
As my first joy was all in you,
So shall my last be found there too,
So long as in me life shall last.)

Perhaps she allowed the troubadour to solace her after Henry had rejected her in favour of 'Fair Rosamond'. Like many other rejected wives Eleanor may have decided that infidelity was a game for four players.

Whatever his mother's conduct, Richard absorbed the ethos of her court with joyous acceptance. He himself won renown as a troubadour, as a knight he was without peer in Christendom. While the young Henry indulged his prowess in tournaments, Richard served his military apprenticeship in real warfare against his mother's turbulent vassals.

Geoffrey was a pale copy of his eldest brother: false, fair, ambitious, and yet basically unserious. Provision was made for him by arranging his marriage to Constance of Brittany, daughter of Duke Conan IV, one of the Breton claimants whom the citizens of Nantes had rejected in favour of the elder Geoffrey, Henry II's brother.

When Henry II met Louis VII at Montmirail in 1169, besides the Becket question, the Plantagenet inheritance was discussed. Louis received the renewed homage of Henry II for his continual domains, and it was officially agreed that young Henry, already married to Margaret of France, should inherit the central bloc of Henry II's lands, for which he too paid homage. Richard, who was to marry Alys, the second daughter of Louis VII by Constance of Castile, did homage for his inheritance of Aquitaine and Poitou. Louis agreed that Geoffrey should have Brittany, which thus became officially part of the Plantagenet domains. The problem of John remained. Henry jokingly referred to him as John '*Sans Terre*' – John Lackland. The name stuck, a perpetual reminder that something would have to be done for him.

Louis VII's position in relation to these immensely powerful vassals had lately improved. At last he had a son. After the death of Constance of Castile he had married a third wife, Adela of Champagne. His efforts to beget a male heir were rewarded, for in 1165 Adela had borne him a son Philippe '*le Dieu-Donné*' – 'the God Given' – better known to posterity as Philip Augustus. On the night of his birth, when Paris was bright with bonfires and noisy with bells, an old woman had prophesied 'By the Grace of God there is born to us this night a king who shall be a hammer to the King of the English.'

After the meeting at Montmirail Henry II must have felt that the future of his empire and his sons was happily secured (apart from the problem of how to provide for John). It is paradoxical that Henry expended so much energy in unifying his domains and simultaneously made elaborate arrangements to partition them after his death. For himself, he desired the consolidation of his power, but he was determined that all his sons should be powerful men when their turn came.

The coronation of the Young King seemed to secure the succession to the English throne, but it precipitated the crisis of the conflict with Becket. Then came the hollow reconciliation at Fréteval, the 'hour of the day which was unimportant as it went by' in which Henry lost his temper, and the martyrdom of the archbishop which followed. It is easy to see Henry's quarrels with Eleanor and with Becket as the causes of his later troubles and his ultimate disaster: the former disunited the Plantagenet family, the latter revealed that Henry was not the invulnerable despot that he appeared to be.

For Becket's death Henry was universally blamed; he became an object of execration throughout Christendom. His domains on the continent were placed under interdict by the Pope; this meant that almost all religious life ceased. The only permitted sacraments were the baptism of infants and the absolution of the dying; none must be denied the chance of entering heaven. But the ordinations, public Masses, marriages and ceremonious funerals ceased. Churches were locked and bells were silent. The withdrawal of the rites of the Church proclaimed the disfavour of God. Henry himself was threatened with excommunication, though Alexander III did not carry out the threat. People flocked to the scene of Becket's martyrdom, where miracles were frequently reported: even a man who had been blinded and castrated claimed to have had his sight and his manhood restored.

Henry responded by discreetly absenting himself from the vicinity of Becket's most passionate sympathizers. Between October 1171 and April 1172 he visited Ireland, to assert his authority over the country which Pope Adrian IV had encouraged him to subjugate in the interests of improving the religious life of the Irish, in a Papal Bull named '*Laudabiliter*' (Papal Bulls being always entitled by their opening words.) It is one of the ironies of history that the unhappy relations of England and Ireland should have been exacerbated by papal encouragement of the English to conquer the Irish in the interests of the Catholic religion, and that the Bull in question should have opened with the word '*Laudabiliter*', which means 'Praiseworthily' . . .

By the time Henry returned, his power in Ireland enhanced, the initial fury against him had begun to abate; he was able to make his peace with the Church.

On 21 May 1172, in the cathedral of Avranches, he acknowledged that though his angry words had occasioned the slaughter of Becket, he had neither commanded it nor rejoiced at it. He performed a public penance; he was scourged, and absolved. It was a more complicated matter to resolve the details of his conflict with Becket. On the issue of 'criminous clerics' Becket won a clear victory; for better or for worse clerics remained immune from punishment by the royal courts. The other disputed matters were resolved as they should have been in the first place, undramatically, and in a spirit of compromise.

Henry's adroitness in avoiding further confrontations once Becket was dead, ensured that though he had won his reconciliation with the Church through public humiliation, he did not lose the battle of 'The Constitutions of Clarendon' in every detail.

However, Henry's public penance at Avranches was performed in the presence of the Young King. The latter, venerating Becket's memory and burning with resentment at the limitation of his own powers, saw his father obliged to humble himself; perhaps he then formed the resolution to humble him still further . . .

In 1173 Raymond V of Toulouse acknowledged both Henrys, father and son, as his suzerains. He had repudiated his wife, Louis VII's sister, and he could no longer look for French support. He paid homage to the greatest power that he recognized.

Raymond, like the Young King, could have been described as 'a prodigy of unfaith'. He took his elder suzerain aside and said that since it was a vassal's duty to give his lord good counsel, he counselled him to beware of his wife and his sons. This proved to be sage advice, even though it was given with the intention of fomenting trouble.

Henry II did not take it as much to heart as he should have done. He had come to the south to meet Humbert III, Count of Maurienne (the area later known as Savoy and Piedmont), who had proposed a marriage between his daughter Alice and Prince John. Count Humbert was poor and in need of strong allies. He was willing that John should be his heir, all he asked was that he should not be John 'Lackland' when he married.

Henry thought that the answer was simple: John should be 'enfeoffed' with (granted as fiefs) three strong castles – Chinon, Loudun and Mirebeau – by his brother the Young King.

This proposal was too much for the younger Henry. It seemed to him that in being asked to grant away three strategic strongholds he was being asked to yield three assurances that his shadowy power would one day become substantial. Young Henry eluded his father and fled to Paris, to complain to and seek assistance from his father-in-law, Louis VII. Richard and Geoffrey were swift to follow him. Eleanor was sufficiently delighted at her second husband's discomfiture to decide to join her sons at her first husband's court. The fifty-two-year-old queen left Poitiers in male disguise, and riding hard for the north she was captured by a group of Henry II's soldiers not far from the borders of the French king's territory. The recompense for her gallant trouble-making was sixteen years of imprisonment.

The revolt of her sons spread like a wind-fanned blaze, but despite the encouragement of Louis VII it was too ill-coordinated to succeed. In the opinion of an eminent historian of the period 'Under skilful control the revolt might have resulted in the ruin of the Angevin Empire for the majority of the leading barons on both sides of the Channel welcomed the opportunity of striking a blow at the King who had laid his hand on their castles and kept them strictly in subjection.'

But, though there were risings in Poitou and Brittany, though Normandy was invaded by Louis and the Young King, though England was invaded by Robert, Earl of Leicester (the son of Henry II's recently dead justiciar) with a band of Flemish mercenaries, and by William the Lion, King of Scots, who hoped to extend his frontier southwards, Henry II was eventually victorious. That England was held for him was in part due to the steady loyalty of Richard de Lucy, the other justiciar who had served Henry throughout the reign, and in part to that of Ranulf Glanville, who was to hold that office in the future.

Henry himself probably imputed his victory partly to his own military skill and that of his loyal supporters, and partly to the intercessions of St Thomas of Canterbury, to whom he turned at the darkest moment of the rebellion. He visited Becket's tomb on 13 July 1174, spent a night in fasting and in prayer and submitted to a scourging by the monks. When he reached London he received the news that the King of Scots had been captured even while he himself was entreating St Thomas' help: it seemed clear proof that his sin had been forgiven, for the tide had turned in his favour and the future now looked bright.

Henry re-crossed the Channel, chased Louis and the Young King back into French territory, made a truce with them, and then pursued Richard into Poitou. By the end of September all was over, and at Montlouis near Tours a peace conference was held on the 30th of the month. Henry was magnanimous. In his love for his sons he dealt generously with them, granting them liberal financial provisions and forgiveness for their rebellion. Yet he could not bring himself to yield them the measure of power which, even though none of them had reached the age of twenty, all felt capable of exercising – as Henry had done successfully when he was a youth. Henry's biographer has shrewdly observed that 'Henry paid dearly for his one failing . . . It was essential for the Angevin empire to be ruled by one absolute monarch if it was to survive the machinations of its enemies. Henry could neither bring himself to delegate that power in an efficient and equitable manner, nor to encourage the princes' interest in affairs other than high politics.'

The princes came away from the peace conference at Montlouis generously provided for, and as powerless as when they had attended it. Their grudge against their father remained. The only one to gain was John: he was to receive the English castles of Nottingham and Marlborough, five castles in Normandy and some valuable estates. He was no longer John Lackland and should be well satisfied.

However, all Henry II's sons had been brought up conversant with the legend that as Satan's descendants they were cursed with diabolical faults; it was impossible for them to be bound by ordinary, human ties of loyalty and affection. Henry himself, nurtured in the same belief, did not expect the experience of defeat to teach them a lesson. In the palace of Winchester he commanded that a mural should be painted which showed four eaglets attacking the parent bird. The smallest was seeking the opportunity to peck out its eyes. Henry was wont to observe that the eaglets were his four sons, and that the youngest, whom he loved the most, would prove the most injurious in the end. It is perhaps significant that a fanciful flight of contemporary etymology suggested that the name of Eleanor – Aliénor in its native form – meant golden eagle (*alie* – eagle, *or* – gold). Perhaps Henry's allegorical picture also carried the implication that his four sons shared the nature of his inimical queen.

While the King's sons were forgiven, and the other leading rebels permitted to make their peace, Eleanor remained imprisoned in courteous but unyielding confinement.

Henry II began to live openly with Rosamond de Clifford, but his happiness was short-lived. She died in 1176, having taken the veil during her last illness at the convent of Godstow.

If her grave, as tradition relates, was carved with the following grim epitaph, it was borrowed from the grave of an early Lombard queen who had borne the same name:

Hic jacet in tumba Rosa *mundi non rosa munda*;
Non redolet sed olet quae redolere solet.

(The rose of the world lies here, an unclean rose
Which now offends that did delight the nose.)

The later 1170s were the years in which Henry II's power was at its height; yet he had lost everything which gives a sweet savour to worldly glory.

Personalities

(left) *Geoffrey Plantagenet, Count of Anjou, the second husband of the Empress Matilda. They were the parents of Henry II, the first of the Plantagenet Kings of England* (MANSELL COLLECTION)

(right) *Henry II, King of England, Duke of Normandy, Count of Anjou and Maine: effigy from his tomb in the Abbey of Fontevrault* (BILDARCHIV FOTO MARBURG)

Details of the effigies of Eleanor and her favourite son from their tombs at Fontevrault; (above) *Eleanor of Aquitaine was married first to Louis VII, King of France, and then to Henry II, King of England;* (below) *Richard Coeur-de-Lion, eldest surviving son of Henry II and Eleanor of Aquitaine* (STUDIO E. M. JANET LE CAISNE)

A drawing of the effigy of Berengaria of Navarre, the neglected wife of Richard Coeur-de-Lion (MANSELL COLLECTION)

The effigy of Isabelle of Angoulême, the second wife of King John, who is buried at Fontevrault with many members of the Plantagenet family (JEAN ROUBIER)

(left) *Henry the Lion, Duke of Saxony, with his wife Matilda Plantagenet, the daughter of Henry II and Eleanor of Aquitaine* (ARCHIV FÜR KUNST UND GESCHICHTE)

(above) *The head of King John, with two attendant saints, a detail from his tomb in Worcester Cathedral* (A. F. KERSTING)

(below) *William Longsword, Earl of Salisbury, an illegitimate son of Hnery II, probably by his favourite mistress, Rosamund de Clifford* (ANTHONY MILES)

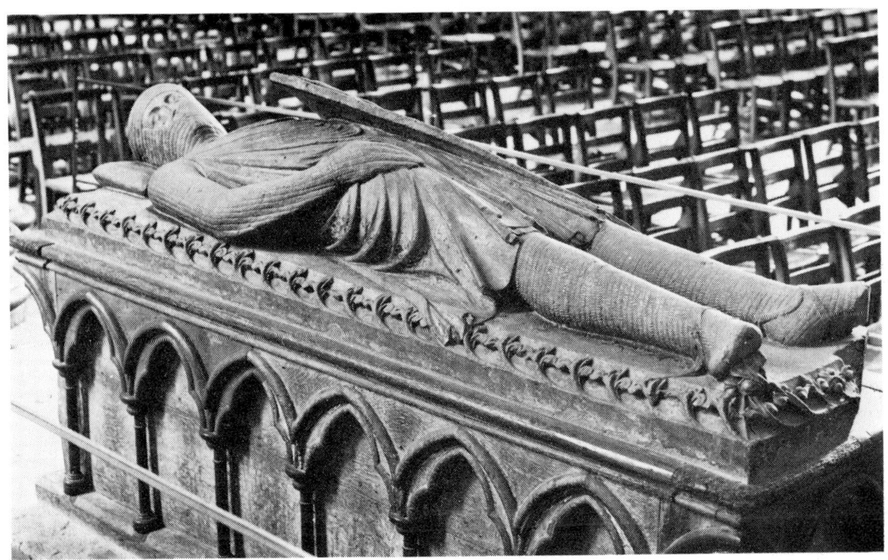

The Great Seals of Louis VII King of France (above) *and Philip Augustus* (centre) *the son of Louis by his third marriage to Adela of Champagne* (GIRAUDON)

(below) *David I* (left) *and Malcolm IV* (right), *Kings of Scots. David I, great-uncle of Henry II, knighted the latter during the struggle with King Stephen. Malcolm IV accompanied Henry II on his unsuccessful expedition against Toulouse in 1159* (THE DUKE OF ROXBURGHE)

A dramatic representation of the murder of St Thomas Becket, in Canterbury Cathedral (MANSELL COLLECTION)

A carving depicting the same event. The clash of personalities between Becket and Henry II made it appear to the popular mind that Becket was defending the Church against secular tyranny. The drama of Becket's martyrdom led to his veneration as a saint whose cult extended from Iceland to Sicily (J. C. D. SMITH)

Head of Hubert Walter, Archbishop of Canterbury, from his tomb in Canterbury Cathedral. Though he was not a great churchman, Hubert Walter was a great administrator and a valued servant of Richard Coeur de Lion (COURTAULD INSTITUTE OF ART)

William Marshal (foreground), *the hero of the age, whose career spans the whole of the period covered by this book. He was received into the order of the Knights Templar on his deathbed, and is buried in the Temple Church in London* (A. F. KERSTING)

V

'Shame on a Conquered King . . .'

Henry (addressing God) *I renounce all*
part in you) no such hands
As yours will have my soul. I'll brand it
For the devil I came from. I'll hurt you
In the centre of your love, as you do me.
My soul is burnt out like the city.
Your eyes can sting like mine, and weep
With the same helpless water.

(Christopher Fry, *Curtmantle*, Act III)

In the castle of Martel in the Dordogne Henry the Young King lay upon a bed of ashes spread on the cold stone floor. A noose of rope was round his neck, to symbolize that he thought himself no better than a common criminal. In the midst of a new rebellion against his father he had been struck down by a fever; burning and shivering with it, he had plundered the richly endowed shrine of St Amadour at Rocamadour to pay his mercenaries. Then repentance had come upon him, with the recognition of the approach of death. He had sent a message to his father, asking his forgiveness, and Henry II had sent him a sapphire ring, as tangible evidence that he granted it.

The Young King lay on his bed of ashes, clad in a hair shirt and his Crusader's cloak; he had taken the Cross and never fulfilled his vow. But his mind was untroubled, for William Marshal had promised to go to the Holy Land in his place. He had given away all his possessions, except the sapphire ring which was on his finger. The monk who had heard his last confession gently asked him if he would like to give it away, and thus achieve the completeness of symbolic poverty.

'I am not keeping this ring out of any desire for possession,' the Young King answered, 'but because I wish my judge to know that my father sent it me as a token of forgiveness.'

He died on 11 June 1183, at the age of 28. Bertran de Born wrote a *planh*, or lament, which commemorated all that was best in him:

> Now every grief and woe and bitterness
> The sum of tears that this sad century's shed,
> Seem light against the death of the Young King,
> And prowess mourns, youth stands sorrowful;
> No man rejoices in these bitter days.
>
> All pride in battle, skill in song and rhyme
> Must yield to sorrow's humble threnody,
> For cruel Death, that mortal warrior,
> Has harshly taken from us the best of knights:
> Beside him Charity itself was mean,
> And in him every noble virtue shone . . .

If Henry II read that lament he might have reflected that his son had possessed every virtue connected with generosity and good fellowship, and none connected with stability or honourable conduct.

'I trust in God for his salvation,' said Henry simply, when William Marshal brought him the news of the Young King's death, adding, 'He has cost me enough, but I wish he had lived to cost me more.'

A kind impulse led him to send the Archdeacon of Wells to break the news to Eleanor. The imprisoned queen astonished the archdeacon by her equanimity. She told him that recently she had had a dream in which she had seen the Young King lying as still as an effigy on a tomb, and wearing two crowns, one of gold and one of light. Without doubt, she said, the crown of light was the crown of immortal life.

The archdeacon went away profoundly impressed that the queen's spiritual life had given her the strength to accept her son's death with the courage of faith. Undoubtedly Eleanor in prison was not indulging herself in fruitless bitterness.

While Eleanor had been held captive the outside world that she had known had witnessed many changes. Bernard of Ventadour had entered a Cistercian monastery; Alice of Maurienne had died, and John had been betrothed to a great English heiress, Havisa of Gloucester; most momentous of all, Louis VII had died, and now his son Philip Augustus sat on the throne of France, dreaming dreams of future greatness.

It was quite a long time since one of Louis VII's courtiers had seen Philip sitting on the ground, gazing into space and chewing the tip of a twig, and had asked him what he was thinking about so deeply. Philip had replied that he was wondering if he could ever make France as great as it had been in the days of Charlemagne. He was still pondering the same question.

Henry II was fifty when the Young King died, but of course men had tended to refer to him as the Old King, if only to differentiate them. However it was undeniable that he was beginning to look like an old king. Despite a frugal diet and hard exercise, he was losing a long battle against corpulence. He was frequently racked by unspecified illnesses.

After the Young King's death the Old King had to face all over again the problem of the division of the Angevin Empire when he himself was dead. It was obvious that Richard must take Young Henry's place as heir to England, Normandy, Anjou and Maine. Geoffrey's future was settled in Brittany by his marriage with Constance. John could be given a truly princely inheritance if he were to receive Aquitaine, acknowledging Richard as his suzerain.

This equitable proposition showed that Henry II had learned nothing from the troubles of the past decade: as before, he strove to do his best for his sons, without regard for their own desires. Richard had no more wish than his elder brother to yield anything to John, the resented paternal favourite. More than that, Aquitaine was the background of Richard's childhood, and in 1172 he had been solemnly invested with the ducal symbols of earthly power and heavenly grace: the coronet, the banner of St Hilaire and the ring of St Valerie. His mother remained duchess and he became duke, an anomalous situation which left no room for John. Richard was not going to give up his duchy; he had been fighting to keep order there ever since his mother had been imprisoned. He refused to be a part to his father's scheme, successfully resisting his efforts to implement it by force.

It was at this point that Philip of France, brooding in silence the problem of his aggrandizement, saw his way forward. If the Plantagenets fought among themselves, it should be his part to keep them fighting, and to gather up the spoils of battle.

He claimed that the Norman Vexin, the dowry of Margaret of France, should have been restored to him on the death of the Young King. Then he agreed that it should become the dowry of his other half-sister Alys, who was to marry Richard. He was probably already aware that there was an impediment to this marriage, for he waited until 1187, and then demanded the restoration of both his sister and the Vexin.

What was the impediment? There was an ugly rumour that Alys of France who had been handed over to Henry II on her betrothal to Richard, had been seduced by Henry, and that Richard was therefore justly reluctant to marry her. But also, Richard was intrinsically reluctant to marry: for him, no woman was worthy of attention except his mother. He seized upon the rumour as an excuse to avoid marriage, and possibly he assisted in spreading it.

Philip, in pursuance of his own demands, invaded Angevin territory and besieged the town of Châteauroux. Henry and Richard came to meet him, and negotiated a truce. Philip, skilfully seeking an opportunity to exploit the latent hostility between father and son, invited Richard to return with him to Paris, where, to the world's astonishment, they not only feasted in perfect amity, but slept together. Susceptible to each other's charms they may have been, but each no doubt supposed the other to be his dupe. Philip's intention was to poison Richard's mind against his father; Richard's was to woo Philip's alliance against Henry. For Richard's latest fear was that Henry intended to make John his principal heir in his place. Philip endorsed his fears. The warrior's intelligence was at the mercy of the politician's . . .

Far away from these scenes of conflict and intrigue, a great battle was fought on 4 July 1187. At Hattin, not far from the Sea of Galilee, the defending army of the Kingdom of Jerusalem was annihilated by Al-Malik al Nasir Salah ad-Din Yusuf, a Moslem hero and a military genius, known in Christendom as Saladin. On 2 October his army entered and occupied the city of Jerusalem, and the Holy Places, together with the greatest relic of the Christian world, the True Cross, fell into infidel hands. The Crusader kingdom, but for its coastal cities of Tyre, Tripoli and Antioch, and a sprinkling of inland strongholds, had fallen. The disaster was blamed to some extent upon Henry II.

In 1185 King Baldwin IV of Jerusalem, the grandson of King Fulk and Queen Melisande, lay dying of leprosy. A powerful embassy was sent to solicit the aid of Baldwin's kinsman Henry II. Heraclius, Patriarch of Jerusalem, set out accompanied by the Grand Masters of the Knights Templar and the Knights Hospitaller. These two orders of military monks had been founded in the early twelfth century, the one to care for the pilgrims and the other to protect the Holy Places. Both followed the profession of arms, and their members were knights who took the religious vows of poverty, chastity and obedience. They lived in celibate communities known as 'commanderies', the Hospitallers subject to the Augustinian rule and the Templars to the Benedictine. Their Grand Masters were personages of international influence.

The Grand Master of the Templars died on the journey to England, but the Grand Master of the Hospitallers and the Patriarch Heraclius arrived to be received by Henry II at Reading. They brought letters from the pope – now Lucius III – in support of their appeal, and though Baldwin IV had an heir, they offered the throne of Jerusalem to Henry himself, who of all Christian kings might have the strength to defend it, or if he refused it, to his one available son, John.

On his knees John begged his father to be permitted to accept the crown of the Crusader kingdom; here was an inheritance worthy of Plantagenet ambition, unaffected by the perennial infighting. Henry refused his entreaties. He had another plan for John, which belonged within the framework of the Angevin empire; John should become Lord, or perhaps King, of Ireland.

It was upon this revelation of the blind selfishness and self-destructiveness of the Angevins' ambitions that the Patriarch Hereclius is reported to have exclaimed '*De diabolo venerunt, et ad diabolo ibunt*' – 'From the Devil they came to the Devil they will return'–a castigation which Richard adopted as a boast.

Ranulf Glanville took the Cross, on hearing the plea of Heraclius to which his king turned deaf ears. Henry II and Philip of France took the Cross after Jerusalem had fallen, too late and with too little enthusiasm to help the Christians in the east. Richard responded to the fall of Jerusalem with all the ardour which characterized him. His was one of those natures which see-saws perpetually between sin and repentance, emotionally ready to obey the summons to the Crusade: 'O mighty soldier, O man of war, you now have a cause for which you can fight without endangering your soul; a cause in which to win is glorious, and for which to die is but gain . . . Take the sign of the Cross. At once you will have indulgence for all the sins which you confess with a contrite heart . . . if you wear it with humility you will find that it is worth the Kingdom of Heaven.'

Richard was determined to defend the Christians' possession of the Holy Land, both for military glory and for his soul's salvation. But he would not go until he was sure that he had secured his rights as the principal heir of the Angevin possessions; in this frame of mind he remained his father's enemy and King Philip's pawn.

Richard may have had reason to suspect that his father's particular love for John might redound to his own disfavour. Henry II had made no move to have Richard crowned as his successor, though he had previously made such efforts to secure the succession through the coronation of the Young King. This alone suggested that he might be considering promoting John in preference to Richard. (Geoffrey was beyond consideration, for he had been accidentally killed at a tournament in 1186, leaving a posthumous son, Arthur of Brittany.) Philip of France would have encouraged Richard in this view, for he himself had been crowned before the death of his father Louis VII in 1180, and he would have been at pains to stress the importance of the rite.

A series of revolts which broke out in Aquitaine and Toulouse shortly after Richard had taken the Cross were believed to have been instigated by Henry, with the intention of keeping Richard distracted by minor troubles from either of his major ambitions. Philip of France, probably by prior arrangement with Richard, offered to arbitrate, and upon Henry's refusal, invaded his domains once more, and now successfully captured Châteauroux.

In the summer of 1188 Henry crossed the Channel for the last time from England to the Continent, bringing a mixed force which included Welsh mercenaries. Desultory fighting and fruitless parleying occupied the autumn.

A peace conference at which Henry, Richard and Philip were present was held at Bonmoulins on 18 November 1188. Here Richard demanded immediate recognition as his father's principal heir, and the homage of all Henry's vassals. Since Richard's demands were seconded by Philip, Henry would have felt bound to refuse them lest he should have been appearing to concede them under the compulsion of French power. He refused, whereupon Richard – doubtless by previous agreement – sank to his knees before Philip of France and offered him homage for all the Angevin domains on the Continent. He left Bonmoulins in Philip's company.

'Henry had two determined adversaries now,' his biographer has observed, 'one attacking his empire with the object of fragmenting it, the other intent on extracting as large a concession of power within it as he could get.' Whether the former, Philip, or the latter, Richard, were the more formidable mattered little so long as they acted in concert.

A truce was negotiated over the winter, while a papal legate, John of Agnani, endeavoured to formulate peace terms, in the interests of hastening the departure of the new crusade. Another conference was held at La Ferté-Bernard, on 4 June 1189, at which it was proposed that Henry, Philip, Richard and John should depart together on the Crusade; all thereby being prevented from making mischief behind one another's backs. Henry refused, showing himself as unable to compromise as he had ever been.

He even proposed that Alys of France should be married to John instead of Richard; it must have seemed that his infatuation for his youngest son had robbed him of his judgment. No clearer statement of his intention to disinherit Richard in favour of John could have been made.

Philip, apparently supporting Richard even as he manipulated the Plantagenets like chess pieces, indignantly refused to entertain the proposal, and suggested that John of Agnani must be in the pay of Henry II to be a party to such an idea. The conference ended in uproar, and once more Philip and Richard departed together. The outbreak of war followed swiftly.

Henry fell back on Le Mans, while Richard and Philip together invaded Maine. Stronghold after stronghold fell to them, almost without resistance. They came on, to lay siege to Le Mans itself. Henry ordered the destruction of the bridge over the river Huisne, which would allow the besiegers an easy approach to the city, and he had sharpened stakes driven into the river bed at every place where he believed it could be forded.

He was reconnoitring outside the walls of the city on 12 June, when he and his escort saw Richard's soldiers taking soundings of the river bed with their lances, and slowly but surely making a successful crossing.

Henry ordered the suburbs outside the south gate of the city to be set on fire, to impede the besiegers' advance. But, as though the elements themselves had turned against him, the wind changed, blowing great sheets of flame over the city walls. Soon Le Mans was afire, and Henry, who had retreated into the city through the south gate, fled from it to the north.

His retreat was covered by William Marshal, who having made his pilgrimage to the Holy Land, served the elder Henry Plantagenet as faithfully as he had served the younger. Richard, who in the excitement of pursuing his hated father had not even paused to put on his armour, suddenly found himself facing the point of William Marshal's lance. He shouted to him:

'By God, Marshal, do not kill me! It would not be a good deed, because I am unarmed!'

'I shall not kill you,' William answered. 'I leave that to the Devil.'

Changing his aim with perfect mastery, he impaled Richard's horse on his lance; and leaving the pursuers to gather round the unhorsed prince, he galloped after his king.

Henry had paused on a hilltop, to look back at the burning city of Le Mans, his birthplace. In the bitterness of despair he addressed God blasphemously:

'Since thou, O God, to crown me with confusion and increase my dishonour, hast basely taken from me this day the city I have loved best in all the world, wherein I was born and bred, and my father is buried . . . I also will surely recompense Thee as far as I am able, by withholding from Thee that which Thou lovest best in me.'

It was the descendant of Satan, not the Christian king who spoke, denying God the redemption of his soul.

Henry, who had retreated to the great castle of Chinon, met Philip of France and Richard for the last time on 4 July, in the open country between Tours and Azay-le-Rideau. His mind, which had surely lost its acuteness at the time of the meeting at La Ferté-Bernard, was utterly numbed by his misfortune. His physical condition had deteriorated so obviously that the King of France took off his cloak and spread it on the ground for his enemy to sit on. Henry proudly refused, though he had to be supported on his horse while he listened to the humiliating peace terms which Richard and Philip imposed upon him: he was to do homage to Philip, to surrender Alys, to cause his vassals to do homage to Richard, to depart on the Crusade by the following Lent, to pay Philip an indemnity of 20,000 marks, and to surrender specified strongholds in pledge of his word. All this he promised, though he whispered to Richard as he gave him an insincere kiss of peace, 'God grant that I may not die until I have had my revenge on you.'

Utterly humiliated, sick in body and in soul, he returned to Chinon, like an old lion, going to its lair to die.

During the last few days John, who had been with his father at Le Mans, had unaccountably disappeared; but Henry had two faithful attendants, William Marshal, the exemplar of loyalty, and Geoffrey of Lincoln, one of Henry's two acknowledged bastards who may have been the sons of Rosamond de Clifford.

On 5 July Henry was obviously dying. Still fighting for his life, he said to Geoffrey:

'If, God willing, I recover from this sickness, I will certainly give you all that a father should and make you among the greatest and most powerful men in my domains. What I cannot repay now, should I die, may God repay you.'

If God turned a deaf ear to Henry's desire to be revenged on Richard, He heard his prayer for Geoffrey. The bastard Geoffrey Plantagenet became Archbishop of York, and he proved to be an excellent choice.

King Henry had one more wound to endure before his death: it was the intelligence that John had disappeared to join his fortunes with those of Philip and Richard. Despite the mural in the palace of Winchester, and despite his comments on it, the knowledge of John's ultimate treachery proved to be the *coup de grâce* for his father.

'Now let everything go as it will,' the king groaned aloud, 'I care no longer for myself or anything else in the world.'

His last audible words were:

'Shame, shame on a conquered king.'

Some of the king's servants managed to strip his corpse after it had been laid ceremoniously in the chapel of Chinon Castle. No doubt they feared that their chances of receiving anything from the victors would be slender. It remained for the few who had proved faithful to see that King Henry was decently buried. A knight of the king's household named William de Trihan covered the naked corpse with his cloak, a short riding cloak, which, it was noticed, made Henry's nickname of 'Curtmantle' peculiarly appropriate at his ending.

William Marshal and Geoffrey the Bastard were able to make good the despoilment which had occurred while their backs were turned. They found a crown, sceptre and ring, possibly borrowed from a religious statue, to array the corpse with a semblance of royalty. It was carried from Chinon to Fontevrault for burial.

The abbey of Fontevrault, much favoured by the Plantagenets, was a rare type of foundation, a double community of monks and nuns, rigidly segregated, and ruled by an abbess. Its members were all aristocratic, and many were royal. It grew in time to be a royal charnel.

When Henry II died, humbled by his spoilt sons and his ambitious young suzerain King Philip, he was widely hated, largely because he had imposed order throughout his domains without fear or favour. Later the chronicler William of Newburgh put his achievements in perspective:

'Ungrateful men, and those bent on evil courses talked incessantly of the wickedness of their own monarch and would not endure to hear good spoken of him. To such men in particular the hardships of the days that followed alone brought understanding. Indeed, the evils that we are now suffering have revived the memory of his good deeds, and the man, who in his own times was hated by many, is now declared everywhere to have been an excellent and beneficial ruler.'

PART TWO

King Richard I Coeur de Lion

. . . the kind of man he was can be seen from the effigy at Fontevrault . . . Looking down at that noble battered face, one feels instinctively the presence of greatness. The set of the head on the thick sturdy neck, the wide shoulders, the deep chest are eloquent of masculine energy and strength. The face, in its stern concentration, with its splendid brow, finely formed nose, high cheekbones and firm small mouth with pouting underlip, combines in a unique degree the qualities of warrior and poet.
(Philip Henderson, *Richard Coeur de Lion*, Prologue)

I
The Hero King

His valour could no throng of mighty labours quell . . . no abyss of the deep, no mountain heights . . . no fury of the winds, no clouds with showers drunk, no thunders, dreadful visitations, no murky air. None of these dangers prevented him from making trial of the prowess of the Sicilians, of Cyrprus, of Saladin, of the Pagan nations in arms.

(The Chronicle of Roger of Howden)

Richard Plantagenet came to Fontevrault, where his father's body lay in state. It was reported that he stood gazing at the corpse for the length of time that it takes to say a *Paternoster* ('Our Father'), and then turned away. While he stood there the corpse bled from the nose, to the horror of all beholders; it was a widely held superstition that a corpse would bleed in the presence of its murderer. If Richard had not murdered his father he had at least hounded him to death. However, he turned from the corpse without emotion, and once again found himself face to face with William Marshal.

'Marshal,' he said, 'the other day you sought to kill me. You would have done it, too, if I had not turned aside your lance with my hand.'

'My Lord,' replied William, 'I never sought to kill you. If that had been my aim, I am strong enough to direct my lance where I please. I could have killed you as easily as I killed your horse. What is more, if I had killed you I would have done no wrong, and I would not now reproach myself for having done anything sinful or wicked.'

'Marshal,' said Richard, 'I pardon you, and in my heart there is no rancour.'

'Thank you, my Lord,' said William Marshal simply, 'I have never desired that you should die.'

Richard was essentially fair-minded, and often magnanimous. William Marshal had faithfully served Richard's elder brother, the Young King, and had remained with Henry II while almost all had deserted him; now that Richard was king the same unshakeable loyalty was at his disposal, and he was wise to claim it. But he did more than set aside resentment that William Marshal had publicly humiliated him in defence of his father; he honoured the promise that his father had made to give William a great heiress in marriage. She was Isobel de Clare, daughter of the Earl of Pembroke. William who had possessed nothing but the gains resulting from his skill in tournaments, became Earl of Pembroke in right of his wife, and one of King Richard's greatest vassals.

In the meantime Richard sent William Marshal back to England with orders for the immediate release of Queen Eleanor, who was to govern England until his arrival. Eleanor remarked that 'prisons were distasteful to men and that to be released therefrom was a most delightful refreshment to the spirit', and ordered a general amnesty. It was a superbly skilful bid to win popularity for the new king, even if it meant, in the words of a contemporary, that 'transgressors were free to transgress more confidently in the future'.

Eleanor was now sixty-seven years old, but imprisonment had neither embittered her nor prematurely aged her. Admittedly, her confinement had not denied her exercise, and she had enjoyed brief glimpses of liberty when Henry had required her presence on state occasions. But Eleanor's true element was the world of action, and she rejoiced to have a part in it once more. Besides, her life had been given a new purpose: her favourite son had become the master of the Angevin Empire, and she was resolved to serve, enhance and share his glory.

Richard I, whose faults were many, was a king who could inspire adoration. He stood over six feet tall, which gave him an especially kingly presence in an age when the average height of a man was several inches less than it is now. He had the proportions of a warrior, and he was strikingly handsome, with brilliant red-gold hair and steely grey eyes.

On 3 September 1189, he entered Westminster Abbey to be crowned King of England. The procession of great lords walking before him with the regalia included his brother John and David, Earl of Huntingdon, brother of the King of Scots, carrying the Swords of State, William Marshal carrying the Sceptre-with-the-Dove, and William de Mandeville, Earl of Essex, bearing the Crown, on its cushion.

Richard knelt before the High Altar, and swore on a copy of the Gospels to live his life peaceably and honourably, to reverence God and the Church, to do justice to his people, to eliminate evil customs and to ratify and enact good laws. Then Baldwin, Archbishop of Canterbury, in the presence of many other prelates, both English and Norman, anointed the king – which was the rite which gave his kingship its sacred aspect – and then commanded him not to accept the Crown unless it was his true intention to keep his oath.

'With God's help I shall observe it without deception,' Richard answered.

So the great Crown of England was set on his head, and two of his barons stood at either side of him supporting the weight of the Crown while Mass was celebrated, their action symbolizing that the king's authority was supported by his vassals.

During the Mass, although it was noon and the sombre interior of the abbey was lit with shafts of sunlight, a bat was seen zig-zagging in its strange erratic flight around the head of the king. All present saw it as an evil omen, and some perhaps remembered the bleeding of his father's corpse.

No misfortune befell Richard that day, but the rejoicings were marred by an act of collective savagery. The crowd outside the palace of Westminster, probably somewhat drunk as the day drew to its end, turned upon and killed a deputation of Jews from the city of London, who were trying to bring gifts to the new king. Richard was enraged, for the Jews were supposed to enjoy royal protection. (This was for reasons not of tolerance but of expediency, since they practised the useful profession of money-lending; 'usury', or lending at interest, was forbidden to Christians.) However, the new wave of crusading ardour brought with it a fury of anti-Semitism, and massacres of Jews took place not only in London but also at King's Lynn, Norwich, Lincoln, Stamford and York. Many men who intended to go on Crusade would have thought that stealing money from Jews was a respectable method of financing their journey, and killing the Jews was often the concomitant of looting their property.

The Crusade was uppermost in King Richard's mind. Since before his father's death he had burned with impatience to fulfil his vow, for he was determined upon the recovery of the Holy Places from Infidel hands. For an enterprise on such a scale he required vast sums of money. It has been said aptly enough that he 'used England as a bank on which to draw and overdraw in order to finance his ambitious exploits abroad . . . that the country stood and survived the strain is the highest proof of the soundness of Henry II's constructive work.'

Though Richard had been born in Oxford, he had spent little time in England; his childhood memories belonged to the city of Poitiers and the countryside of Poitou and Aquitaine. England served two purposes for him: to give him his kingship and to supply his needs.

In thinking of means to supply the needs of the Crusade he showed a fertile imagination. Offices of state were put up for sale, which was not in itself unusual, but Richard thought of the profitable scheme of dismissing officials who had served his father, and then allowing them to re-purchase their appointments. In his enthusiasm to raise money Richard is reported to have remarked 'I would sell London, if I could find a purchaser.'

One man who was not allowed to buy his way into Richard's favour was his father's justicar, Ranulph Glanville; perhaps he was excepted because he had been Queen Eleanor's gaoler. The king took a heavy fine from him without restoring him to office; Glanville decided to fulfil his Crusader's vow, and died on the Crusade.

However, Richard had to appoint justiciars to rule in his absence. Archbishop Baldwin of Canterbury, whom he might have chosen, was to accompany him on Crusade. He chose two other ecclesiastics, Hugh de Puiset, Bishop of Durham, an aristocrat of princely presence, and William de Longchamp, Chancellor and Bishop of Ely, a man of humble origins who had the added disadvantage of being short and ugly. They were an ill-chosen pair, for though both were loyal to the king there was a bitter antipathy between them. Longchamp was extremely ambitious and self-assertive. According to a contemporary 'the laity found him more than a King, the clergy more than a Pope, and both an intolerable tyrant.'

The trouble between them was in the future when the king prepared to leave England. Before his departure he was chiefly concerned to prevent his brother John from making mischief in his absence. Richard had an affection for John, but he rightly regarded him as entirely untrustworthy. Nonetheless, he treated him with great generosity. John had become Earl of Gloucester in right of his wife Havisa, he was also created count of Mortain in Normandy, and he was granted the royal revenues of six English counties: Derby, Nottingham, Dorset, Somerset, Devon and Cornwall.

Having provided John with a princely inheritance, Richard began to wonder if he had given his brother the means to become dangerously powerful. Half-repenting, he made John swear to remain out of England for a period of three years, which was probably the length of time which he estimated his own absence might be. John apparently prevailed on his mother to persuade Richard to change his mind, for John had scarcely sworn the oath when he was released from it again at Queen Eleanor's request.

The scene in England was thus set for trouble by the time Richard was ready to leave for the Holy Land.

Richard sailed out of Dover on 11 December 1189. He had gathered a mighty fleet of more than a hundred ships, and having disembarked to go overland to meet Philip of France, he ordered the fleet to sail around the coast and enter the Mediterranean, to join him at Marseilles.

Evidently he was determined that the behaviour of his sailors should be worthy of a religious enterprise, for he issued stern ordinances to that effect:

> Anyone who slays a man on board ship shall be thrown into the sea lashed to the corpse; if on land he shall be buried in the ground tied to the corpse. Anyone convicted by lawful witnesses of striking another so as to draw blood shall lose his hand; but if he strikes with his hand without drawing blood he shall be dipped three times in the sea.

Violent men were warned beforehand of the penalties which their quarrels might incur; but in devising the penalties Richard revealed the vein of cruelty in his nature.

When he reached Tours Richard received the symbolic pilgrim's staff which was presented to every Crusader as the emblem of the central purpose of his journey. He leant upon the staff and it snapped beneath his weight. This chance seemed, to superstitious eyes, to be the third ill-omen of his reign.

At Vézelay he met Philip Augustus, and there they learned that the Emperor Frederick Barbarossa, who had taken the Cross and had set out several months previously to march overland with his army to Palestine, had been drowned in the river Calycadrus in Asia Minor. With the imperial army left leaderless and liable to disintegration, the success of the Third Crusade became the joint responsibility of the kings of England and France.

Of their earlier intimacy not a shadow remained. In the astute and patient mind of Philip Augustus, Richard had taken Henry II's place as the enemy whose power must be eroded by every available means. He was too astute to reveal overt enmity, but the fact that he had required of Richard the indemnity of 20,000 marks which the dying Henry II had promised to pay him, had been sufficient to arouse Richard's suspicions. The new relationship of Richard and Philip was guarded; gradually it became inimical. However at Vézelay, in anticipation of the success of their Crusade, they agreed to divide the spoils of war equally between them.

On 4 July 1190, the third anniversary of the battle of Hattin, they struck their vast camp, which had been likened to a city of pavilions, and began their march south. Philip was to make his way to Genoa, there to hire ships to transport his army to the Holy Land; Richard was to go to Marseilles, his rendezvous with his fleet.

He found no ships at Marseilles; his fleet had been delayed in Portugal. In a fury of impatience at the thought that his long-deferred Crusade might be deferred yet longer, he hired an equally vast fleet to transport his army on its way, and then set sail leaving orders that his own ships should follow down the coast of Italy.

On the voyage he paused to visit the medical school at Salerno, the centre of the most experimental medicine in Christendom. Richard was as interested in the skills of curing as in those of killing. Indeed, there was very little accessible knowledge or experience that did not invite him, for curiosity was perhaps one of the strongest impulses of his nature.

Late in September he arrived at Messina, where he expected to find his sister Joanna reigning as Queen of Sicily. Instead he arrived in time to save her from a desperate reversal of fortune. Her husband William II 'the Good' had died the previous year, and the throne of Sicily was claimed by his aunt Constance who was married to the new Holy Roman Emperor, Henry VI. The idea of imperial domination was repugnant to the Sicilians, who preferred as their king William II's illegitimate cousin, Tancred of Lecce. On becoming king, Tancred had thrown Joanna into prison.

Richard's coming must have seemed like a miracle to his sister. He came splendidly, deliberately intending to overawe the Sicilians:

> Around the ships the sea boiled as the oarsmen drove them onwards. Then, with trumpet peals ringing in their ears, the onlookers beheld what they had been waiting for: the King of England, magnificently dressed and standing on a raised platform, so that he could see and be seen.

As soon as he had discovered the situation in Messina, Richard forced Tancred to release his sister. The initially excited populace soon proved to be suspicious and unfriendly, and Richard, impatient of non-cooperation in such matters as supplies of food to his army at fair prices, took the city by storm. He occupied it throughout the winter, while he negotiated with Tancred the return of Joanna's dowry and the payment to himself of William II's rich legacy to Henry II, which had been intended as a contribution to the Crusade.

Philip Augustus, who had also made landfall at Messina, contrived to poison the relations of Tancred and Richard, where he saw opportunity. He raised once again the question of Richard's long-delayed marriage to Alys of France, and Richard finally refused her, offering to produce witnesses to the fact that she had been his father's mistress. Philip agreed to the repudiation of his half-sister, in return for a payment by Richard of 10,000 marks. Possibly Richard's excuse was grounded in truth, for Alys was subsequently married to a mere knight, a suitable match for a king's erstwhile mistress, though scarcely for a daughter of France.

While he was at Messina, Richard summoned an assembly of prelates, before whom he appeared half-naked, as a penitent, and confessed that he had sinned against nature. No doubt his extravagant repentance was intended as a preparation for his marriage, for while he was extricating himself from his betrothal to Alys he must have known that his mother had gone to Navarre to negotiate his marriage to Berengaria, the daughter of King Sancho VI of Navarre. It was a politic match which would secure the southern border of Aquitaine and, even if Richard was reluctant to marry, he accepted that it was his duty as a king to do so.

Despite his confession, which may indicate the direction of his sexual preference, since it was repeated in 1195, Richard proved that he was not inflexibly averse to women: he acknowledged a bastard son named Philip, who occupies a larger place in Shakespeare's *King John* than in history itself.

At the end of March 1191 Eleanor of Aquitaine, bringing the Princess of Navarre, arrived in Messina. The luckless princess who was to be Richard's wife was described as a 'lady of beauty and good sense'. It seems that she never succeeded in winning Richard's affections; her good sense is perhaps best shown by the fact that no enmity is recorded between her and Queen

Eleanor, whose occupation of Richard's heart left little room for others.

The tireless Eleanor remained four days in Sicily, committed Berengaria to the care and company of Joanna, and sailed away to Italy, to bully the pope on Richard's behalf.

Richard did not marry Berengaria immediately, for the penitential season of Lent had begun, and during its forty days marriages were not permitted. He set sail from Sicily on 10 April 1191, planning to marry in the Holy Land. Philip Augustus had sailed before him, impelled not only by the motives of the Crusade, but by a natural wish not to see the princess who was to take the place of Alys as Queen of England.

Violent storms drove the ship which carried Berengaria and Joanna aground on the southern coast of Cyprus, and Joanna, who had learned caution from her experiences with Tancred, refused an invitation to land issued by the ruler of the island, Isaac Comnenus, who called himself emperor.

Isaac was a kinsman of the Greek royal house which ruled the Byzantine Empire from Constantinople. He had arrived in Cyprus with forged papers purporting to appoint him the island's governor, and having established his power had assumed the style of emperor. It was unfortunate for him that he had both sought to secure himself against the government in Constantinople, which he had betrayed, by allying himself with Saladin, and that he had sought to decoy the sister and the betrothed of the King of England to accept his dubious hospitality in Cyprus.

Richard could have rescued Joanna and Berengaria from their half-wrecked ship without troubling Isaac Comnenus, but his military sense told him that it would be folly to sail onwards to the Holy Land, leaving an ally of his principal enemy in his rear.

Having landed in Cyprus and gained a preliminary victory, Richard married Berengaria of Navarre in the Chapel of St George at Limassol on 12 May. Far away from the country which gave her regality, she was crowned Queen of England by a Norman prelate, John, Bishop of Evreux.

After his wedding, Richard turned his attention to the conquest of Cyprus. Though Richard was a commander of genius, he might have wasted many months and jeopardized his reputation in attempting the conquest of such a difficult terrain, had not two valuable hostages fallen into his hands. The wife and daughter of Isaac Comnenus were captured by Guy of Lusignan, who called himself King of Jerusalem, since he was married to the heiress of the Crusader kingdom. But Guy was a baron of Poitou, and Richard's vassal; his captives were Richard's captives.

Upon the capture of his wife and daughter Isaac Comnenus surrendered to Richard, requesting only that he might not be disgraced by being put in irons. Richard's cruel fashion of granting his request was to have chains of silver forged for him.

Richard swiftly set up his own administration in Cyprus, to secure the island as a supply base for the Crusaders. After the many interruptions of his voyage Richard was consumed with impatience to reach the Holy Land at last, and as eager as a lover to get to grips with Saladin, a worthy enemy whose reputation matched his own.

Already Richard was a hero king whose fame had been enhanced by the conquest of Cyprus; it was very easy to forget how much the rapidity of that conquest owed to Guy of Lusignan's capture of the Comnenus ladies.

Map showing Second and Third Crusades

II
In the Holy Land

O, still, methinks, I see King Richard stand
In his gilt armour stain'd with Pagan's blood,
Upon a galley's prow, like war's fierce God,
And on his crest a crucifix of gold!

(Anthony Mundy, *The Downfall of Robert, Earl of Huntingdon*)

On 8 June 1191 King Richard's fleet approached the port of Acre. It was held by a Moslem garrison and besieged by Guy of Lusignan, who had initiated the siege before temporarily joining King Richard in Cyprus. Guy's army was in turn threatened by a relieving force led by Saladin himself.

Guy of Lusignan was a character reminiscent of King Stephen. He was too guileless a man to assert his authority over wily and ambitious subjects; yet he was a good knight and a brave soldier. Though hard-pressed by Saladin, Guy was holding his own when the fleet of Philip Augustus arrived. French support proved ineffectual, however, and the siege was still dragging on inconclusively when Richard's fleet came in sight of Acre.

Richard had been at odds with Philip before he left Sicily, but he had experienced his first taste of the disharmony of the Crusaders in the East when, upon reaching the Holy Land on 6 June, he had expected to be welcomed into the city of Tyre. Instead, he had been refused entry by the Lord of Tyre, Conrad of Montferrat, a nobleman of German–Sicilian extraction, who was contesting with Guy of Lusignan the somewhat chimerical kingship of Jerusalem.

Guy's wife, Sibylla of Jerusalem, had died in the autumn of 1190, and Conrad of Montferrat had made haste to marry her younger sister, Isabella. He claimed that Guy could no longer call himself King of Jerusalem in right of his wife once his wife was dead; whereas he, Conrad, could claim to be king in right of *his* wife Isabella, the surviving heiress of the kingdom. His claim was both arguable and ingenious. Richard I, however, was the suzerain of Guy of Lusignan, and therefore Conrad prudently excluded him from Tyre.

Unperturbed, Richard had encamped outside Tyre, to allow his men a comforting re-acquaintance with dry land, and had then sailed on, to grapple with the enemy.

The first encounter took place almost at once, below the walls of Acre, where Richard's fleet encountered a supply ship, flying the banner of the King of France. The ship's crew proved to be Moslems, convincingly disguised, and attempting to bring supplies not to Philip of France and Guy of Lusignan, but to the almost starving defenders of the city. The sinking of the Moslem supply ship was Richard's first heroic exploit on reaching the Holy Land.

He went on to besiege Acre with such resolution and skill that on 12 July its garrison surrendered upon stringent conditions: the lives of the defenders were to be spared for a ransom of two hundred thousand gold dinars, and in exchange for fifteen hundred Christian prisoners and the relic of the True Cross.

When the crusading armies occupied Acre an untoward incident occurred, which was to have unhappy consequences for King Richard. On the walls of Acre the banners of three conquering heroes were set up: King Richard of England, King Philip of France and Duke Leopold of Austria. Leopold was the acknowledged leader of the straggling remnant of the imperial Crusade which had set out under Frederick Barbarossa. He lacked the resources of the two kings, and needed a share of the loot of Acre to reward his followers. Richard and Philip, however, had agreed upon an equal division of the spoils of war. Both were resolved to exclude Leopold from the share to which the display of his banner staked a claim; but it was Richard who, with characteristic impetuosity, ordered the banner to be torn down and trampled underfoot. Leopold thenceforward nourished against him a grudge which in due course he found an opportunity to avenge.

After the capture of Acre, Philip, whose health had suffered in the hot climate of the east, announced his intention of going home. In vain Richard, and some of his own followers, urged him to stay; but Philip had other reasons than his health which impelled him to return to France. The death of his uncle the Count of Flanders had left him the heir to a vast territory of which he was anxious to secure possession. Furthermore, he had hopes of pursuing his ambitions against the Angevin Empire by intriguing with Prince John in Richard's absence. On 3 August 1191, less than a month after the capture of Acre, Philip of France abandoned the Crusade and set sail for home.

Richard had very good reason to fear the consequences of Philip's departure.

He was already aware of the troubles which had arisen in England almost as soon as his back was turned. Indeed, from Messina he had despatched Walter of Coutances, Archbishop of Rouen, to attempt to resolve the strife which had broken out between Hugh de Puiset and William de Longchamp, in which Prince John had played the mischief-maker with considerable gusto. John, like everyone else, had a valid viewpoint of his own. Richard had nominated as his heir, in the event of his death on Crusade, not John who felt that he should have been nominated, but his young nephew, Arthur of Brittany.

Hugh de Puiset had fallen into the hands of his cleverer rival, Longchamp, by the time that Walter of Coutances arrived in England. Walter was working to restore harmony when Longchamp overreached himself completely by seizing and imprisoning the newly consecrated Archbishop of York, the bastard Geoffrey Plantagenet. His excuse was that Geoffrey had been ordered to remain out of England for three years (presumably to keep him separated from the trouble-making John, who had been released from the same obligation) and had returned before the expiry of the term. It was in vain that Longchamp sought to justify himself: Geoffrey Plantagenet became in popular esteem a victim of tyranny, and a lesser Becket, suffering in the interests of the Church.

The force of influential opinion approved the arrival of Walter of Coutances, and in due course led to the exile of Longchamp, and favoured the appointment of Walter as chief justiciar. In these upheavals, however, Prince John was not content to remain in the background. According to one contemporary source he began to style himself *Summus Rector Totius Regni*, a circumlocutive way of calling himself regent. His power was certainly in the ascendant, despite Walter of Coutances, by the time that Philip Augustus returned from the Crusade.

It was early in 1192 that Philip proposed a marriage between Alys of France and Prince John, a match which would bring John all the continental domains of the English king, in return for his homage. The proposal to marry her to John was the last employment of Alys of France as a political pawn; it is to be hoped that she eventually found peace and happiness with the unexalted husband who won her. John was prevented from accepting the tempting propositions of Philip by the return to England of Queen Eleanor, who possessed considerable influence over her youngest son, if not the total ascendancy which she enjoyed over Richard.

The condition of England was turbulent, and the result of its internal intrigues was inconclusive, when Richard assumed command of the Third Crusade, after the departure of Philip Augustus.

Despite the groundswell of disquieting news from England, Richard was determined to push onward to his main objective, the recapture of Jerusalem.

A compromise was arranged to satisfy the rival claimants to the kingdom. Guy of Lusignan was to remain King of Jerusalem until his death, upon which the succession was to go to Conrad of Montferrat and his descendants.

Probably the influence of Richard is to be discerned in an arrangement which mirrored that made between King Stephen and his father. Unfortunately the result of the agreement concerning the Crown of Jerusalem proved less satisfactory.

Before Richard began his advance on Jerusalem, the terms of the surrender of Acre awaited conclusion. Saladin may have prevaricated with the intention of delaying Richard's advance, or he may have had difficulty in gathering the two hundred thousand dinars within the agreed month. At all events, Saladin failed to fulfil the terms, and after further negotiations had broken down, on 20 August Richard ordered and witnessed the massacre of two thousand seven hundred Moslem prisoners.

Richard cut short the bargaining, and at the same time ridded himself of the 'useless mouths' which he lacked the resources to feed, by an act of appalling savagery. Saladin distributed the proportion of the ransom money so far collected as a general largesse to his army. The massacre did not destroy Saladin's respect for Richard as a worthy adversary. Each of them regarded the other as a chivalrous and magnanimous enemy; but while chivalry and magnanimity might govern their diplomatic relations at the personal level, larger issues were subject to considerations of expediency.

On the second day after the massacre the crusading army marched out of Acre and began its slow southward advance, clinging to the coast, supplied and supported by the fleet which sailed alongside. From the land the Crusaders were continuously harassed by the attacks of Saladin's light cavalry, squadrons of which appeared and disappeared in a whirlwind of dust, showering the advancing column with a fatal rain of arrows from their light horsemen's bows. These arrows could not penetrate a knight's mail from any great distance, but they slew many horses and unarmed men. Yet slowly the Crusaders pushed on, until Saladin resolved to risk a pitched battle. On 5 September he sent his brother to parley with the English King.

Richard and Saladin never met, yet as time went by, increasingly each loved the idea of the other as the perfect enemy. This is the understandable reaction of two idealists, surrounded by distrust and treachery among the ranks of their fellows.

Saladin's brother, Malek el Adil Saif-ed-Din, whom the Crusaders called Saphadin, a diplomat and warrior who won Richard's regard at first hand, was told on this occasion that all Richard required of Saladin was the surrender of the entire Holy Land. His terms were an invitation to battle.

The battle of Arsuf, on 7 September, was Richard's victory, and the greatest triumph of the Third Crusade; for the invader had taken the measure of the elusive tactics of the enemy, and had beaten them on their own ground.

Three days later Richard's army occupied Jaffa, the port of Jerusalem. Saladin had destroyed the defences of Jaffa to reduce its usefulness, yet strategically the Crusaders occupied a strong position. The question was whether their supplies could be maintained if they turned inland to besiege Jerusalem itself.

The true answer was in the negative, for Richard's supply lines were attenuated and uncertain, Saladin's resources were accessible and secured. Singular feats of arms might deal blows to Saladin's prestige, but in the long run the very existence of the Crusaders' settlements in the Holy Land was in doubt. They were clinging to the edge of the Moslem world, not threatening it with conquest.

Jerusalem was a Holy City to Christians and Moslems alike. It was both the scene of Christ's crucifixion, death and resurrection, and the place from which, according to Moslem belief, Mohammed had ascended to heaven. This holy ground would not change hands lightly.

Richard, enamoured of his noble enemies, suggested that Saladin should bestow the Holy Land upon Saphadin; that Saphadin should marry Joanna; that her dowry should be the coastal strip of the country from Acre to Ascalon, and that Christian pilgrims should have free access to Jerusalem, which should be the capital of the Christian–Moslem kingdom.

Saladin and Saphadin agreed almost incredulously to these terms, wondering perhaps whether Richard was revealing himself as a lunatic or a visionary. Joanna flew into a rage worthy of a descendant of Melusine. Never, she stormed, never in a thousand years would she permit herself to be married to an infidel. Her demonic fury was grounded in soundly Christian prejudice; furthermore she was on firm legal ground. A woman who had been married was not a pawn like an unmarried girl; a widow had the privilege to choose her own second husband. Even Richard Coeur de Lion could not impose his will upon a combination of fury and legality.

Once she had asserted her rights Joanna, who had a Plantagenet's share of ambition, blandly informed her brother that she would marry Saphadin, if he were to become a Christian. But never in a thousand years would a Moslem prince betray his Prophet. Nothing more was heard of the matter.

Richard turned his strategist's mind to the conquest of Jerusalem. During the autumn he began rebuilding for the Crusaders' use the strongholds which Saladin had destroyed, on the route from Jaffa to the Holy City.

With the onset of winter the weather deteriorated. Those hard-bitten defenders of the Crusader kingdom, the Templars and the Hospitallers, members of whose orders had borne the brunt of the fighting at Arsuf, pointed out to Richard the difficulties of maintaining his supplies if he laid siege to a well-defended city which lay many miles inland. He saw the force of this argument, and at last he ordered a retreat from his nearest point of approach to its walls, which was Beit Nuba, twelve miles from Jerusalem.

His decision was probably incomprehensible to the majority of the Crusaders. They had come to capture Jerusalem, they had come within a dozen miles of it, and their commander ordered them to retreat. The Templars and Hospitallers, who had seen the comings and goings of thousands upon thousands of pilgrims, were probably right when they told Richard that the majority of the Crusaders, once they had knelt at the Holy Sepulchre, would go home. The great weakness of the Crusader kings was that the majority of their followers were volunteers who could not be compelled beyond the limits of their own enthusiasm or the influence of their vows. To visit the Holy Places was the summit of the ambitions of many; the future of the Crusader kingdom was beyond the horizon of their vision.

In the opening months of 1192 Richard was occupying his uncomprehending followers in rebuilding the fortifications of Ascalon, the most southerly defensible port which Saladin had destroyed to prevent its use as a base for the Crusaders.

At Ascalon he received alarming news of intrigues between Philip Augustus and Prince John. He resolved that the time had come for his return to England, or at least to Normandy, and he realized that all his battles in the Holy Land would have been worth nothing unless the rivalry between Guy of Lusignan and Conrad of Montferrat were finally resolved. During the last few months events had made it plain that the compromise reached shortly after Richard's arrival had satisfied neither of them.

Richard summoned a great council at Ascalon on 16 April 1192, to think again and make a final and binding choice between the two claimants.

Conrad received the favourable vote and became titular King of Jerusalem. Richard, who had hitherto supported Guy, compensated him for the loss of the kingship by creating him Lord of Cyprus. No doubt Richard felt that once he had sailed for home Cyprus would be a responsibility to him rather than an asset; he could bestow it on Guy with every appearance of magnanimity, and at the same time rid himself of a burden.

Within a short time Guy's fate proved to be the happier. The Lusignan family ruled Cyprus until 1489, but the career of Conrad of Montferrat came to an extraordinary conclusion.

On 28 April the King-elect of Jerusalem encountered two men who appeared to be monks. One of them, to gain his attention, handed him a letter; as he paused to read it, the two of them stabbed him to death. They proved to be followers of Rashid ed-Din Sinan, known as 'The Old Man of the Mountains', the leader of a revolutionary Moslem sect, whose members, the 'Assassins' had a way of dealing with their enemies which has given a common word to several languages.

It has been suggested that 'assassins' originally meant 'takers of hashish', and that it was under the influence of hashish that the fanatical followers of 'The Old Man of the Mountains' were inspired to kill. But exactly how Conrad of Montferrat had happened to be upon the death list of so formidable an enemy, rather than any other of the leading Crusaders, has never been satisfactorily explained. The least dramatic explanation would be that the Assassins succeeded in killing Conrad of Montferrat, and failed with the rest.

The astounding news of Conrad's death was followed by an equally dramatic turn of events. The man who brought the news to Conrad's widow, Isabella of Jerusalem, was Count Henry of Champagne, who was Richard's nephew. (Henry was the son of Marie of Champagne, the elder daughter of Eleanor of Aquitaine by her first marriage.) Isabella promptly married him.

A cheerful doggerel poet who had accompanied the Crusade recorded the event:

> The French delayed not in the least
> But sent straightway to fetch the priest
> And caused the Count to wed the Dame –
> My Soul! I should have done the same . . .

The acquisition by Henry of Champagne of the claim to the shadowy Kingdom of Jerusalem meant that Richard had one more opportunity to attempt the capture of the Holy City. To set his kinsman on the throne would serve both advantage and prestige, and this time no background rivalry would exert its baneful influence.

For a second time Richard approached as close to Jerusalem as Beit Nuba; and for a second time, after agonies of indecision, he turned back. The same conditions existed as had led to failure at his first approach: the difficulties of maintaining supplies brought by sea to besiege an inland city in enemy country. In addition, Richard's own resolution was undermined by further disquieting news from home; if he did not leave the Holy Land very soon it might be too late to save the Angevin Empire from the machinations of John and Philip Augustus.

In great bitterness of spirit, Richard resolved to retreat. A chronicler of the following century told how, riding among the hills beyond Beit Nuba, Richard had caught a distant glimpse of the towers of Jerusalem. Turning aside his head and lifting his shield to cover his eyes, he had wheeled his horse about and cried out 'Sweet Lord, I entreat Thee, do not suffer me to see Thy Holy City, since I am unable to deliver it from the hands of Thine enemies!'

No doubt for a second time Richard's followers experienced a sense of incomprehensible betrayal. Yet somehow the magic of Richard's reputation survived his second failure to approach, let alone to take, Jerusalem. He remained the hero-king.

Perhaps his reputation was saved not only by his personal reputation for heroism, but by the fact that in his retreat he won a final and memorable victory. At the last possible moment he saved Jaffa from falling into the hands of Saladin by attacking the Moslem victors of the siege at the very instant when the Christian garrison, which had already surrendered, was beginning to march out of the town.

On 2 September 1192, Richard concluded with Saladin a three years' truce. It was agreed that the coast from Tyre to Jaffa should remain in the possession of the Crusaders. Saladin gained Ascalon and retained Jerusalem, to which, nonetheless, Christian pilgrims were to be allowed free access.

Richard took ship at Acre and sailed from the Holy Land on 9 October, to meet the next adventure of his ever-eventful life. Saladin died the following spring, leaving Saphadin to take his place as the defender of the interests of Islam.

It is idle yet alluring to speculate what would have happened if Joanna had consented to marry Saphadin. Did Richard's proposal create the possibility of a turning point in history, around which the protagonists chose not to turn?

Crusades

The First Crusade (1096–99) won the city of Jerusalem for Christendom, and established the Crusader kingdoms in the near east. Godfrey de Bouillon, the first Christian ruler of Jerusalem, lays siege to the city (SNARK INTERNATIONAL)

A late medieval illumination of Jerusalem, which was a Holy City to Christians, Moslems and Jews alike (SNARK INTERNATIONAL)

(right) *A representation of the risen Christ, on the reverse of the Great Seal of the kingdom of Jerusalem* (M. E. ARCHIVE)

(left) *The Crusader's goal: the Church of the Holy Sepulchre. Pilgrims' crosses carved on the wall of the Church* (M. E. ARCHIVE)

(below) *The Crusader's return: Crusader's horseshoes nailed as votive offerings on the door of the Church of St Martin, Chablis* (MANSELL COLLECTION)

The Crusader himself: a sculpture from Rheims Cathedral, showing a knight Crusader receiving Holy Communion (JEAN ROUBIER)

The Crusader's adversary: a saracen warrior, armed with a curved sword or 'falchion' and a light bow of the type used by Infidel cavalry to harrass the slower and more heavily armed Christian knights (MANSELL COLLECTION)

An example of the Crusaders' defences) the great fortress of Krak des Chevaliers, built by the Knights Hospitallers (AEROFILMS)

An imaginary encounter between Richard Coeur de Lion and Saladin, from the early fourteenth-century Luttrell Psalter. In reality, Richard and Saladin never met, either in combat or for purposes of diplomacy (RADIO TIMES HULTON PICTURE LIBRARY)

A contemporary portrait of Saladin, by a Persian artist of the Fatimid School (MANSELL COLLECTION)

The site of the battle of Hattin (1187), after which the victorious Saladin recaptured the city of Jerusalem from the Christians (M. E. ARCHIVE)

King Philip Augustus of France leaves the Holy Land (1191). Disunity between the Kings of England and France contributed influentially to the failure of the Third Crusade (RADIO TIMES HULTON PICTURE LIBRARY)

A parley between Christians and Infidels. Warfare was not the whole story of the Crusades: in the intervals of peace the basis of economic and cultural exchanges were laid down (MANSELL COLLECTION)

As a result of cultural exchanges arising from the residence of Westerners in the Near East, Moslem learning began to percolate into Western Europe. In medicine, mathematics, philosophy and natural history the contribution of the Moslem world can scarcely be over-estimated. A page from an Arabic herbal in the Bodleian Library (BODLEIAN LIBRARY, OXFORD)

III
The Lion Enchained

No prisoner can tell his honest thought
Unless he speaks as one who suffers wrong;
But for his comfort he may make a song.
My friends are many, but their gifts are naught.
Shame will be theirs, if, for my ransom, here I lie another year.

(King Richard I, on his captivity)

King Richard had cared passionately about the rescue of the Holy Places, and the failure of the chief purpose of the Crusade caused him sorrow and bitterness almost beyond description. It was a small consolation that a Syrian bishop and a Greek abbot had each given him a piece of ancient wood which purported to be a relic of the True Cross, broken from the principal relic before it fell into Moslem hands.

Richard was not the last religiously inspired Crusader, for many Templars and Hospitallers, and many humble pilgrims, must have shared his devout enthusiasm. But with the exception of Louis IX, King of France, Richard was the last king who might fairly be described as a Christian hero.

The Crusades deteriorated into a struggle to secure control of trade in the east. By the time that the Crusaders, urged on by the aged, blind Doge of Venice, Enrico Dandolo, sacked Constantinople in 1204, any sense of common Christian purpose had been lost. Earlier Crusades had been characterized by deep suspicion between Latin (Catholic) and Greek Orthodox Christians; but it was fortunate for Richard Coeur de Lion that he did not live to see fellow Christians destroying one another. It was with sufficient disappointment that he sailed for home in the autumn of 1192.

Ill luck attended his voyage. Storms separated the king's ship, the *Franche-nef*, from the rest of the fleet. Richard's companions were two noblemen, Baldwin, Count of Béthune and William de L'Etang, two clerics and a group of Templars.

The *Franche-nef* was seen tossing wildly off the Italian coast near Brindisi; it was sighted near Marseilles. Richard hesitated to land anywhere with so few companions. Eventually he transferred from his storm-battered ship to a pirate vessel which had grappled with the *Franche-nef* and then surrendered upon discovering who was her commander. The pirates landed King Richard somewhere between Venice and Aquileia. He decided to cross Europe incognito, calling himself Hugo, a merchant from the Levant; as a precaution he sent to ask for a safe-conduct from the local magnate, Count Mainard of Görtz.

He was told that Count Mainard stared long at the ruby ring which was offered as the price of the safe-conduct; probably it was too grand a gift to have been sent by even the richest of merchants.

'It is not the merchant Hugo who sends me this gift, but King Richard,' said Count Mainard. 'However, in view of the value of this gift, and the high estate of him who honours me with it, I shall send the ring back to him and give him leave to continue his journey.'

Count Mainard of Görtz was a vassal of Leopold of Austria. Richard rode on his way deeply perturbed that his incognito had been penetrated so easily. Royalty is notoriously incompetent at disguising itself, and Richard rightly doubted Count Mainard's intentions.

Sure enough, Count Mainard sent word of his conjecture concerning the merchant's identity to his brother, Frederick of Betesov, through whose town of Freisach Richard would be obliged to pass. Here again Richard was fortunate, for the man whom Frederick sent to apprehend him was a Norman named Roger of Argentan. He had lived in Austria for twenty years and was married to Frederick of Betesov's niece; nonetheless, he could not bring himself to betray the King of England and Duke of Normandy. He threw himself on his knees at Richard's feet and entreated him to ride on his way as fast as he could. Gratefully Richard took his advice and divided his party: Richard, William de L'Étang and a youth who spoke German rode on separately, leaving Count Baldwin and the Templars for Roger of Argentan to bring before his master. Roger was thus able to assure Frederick of Betesov that his brother must have been mistaken. Baldwin of Béthune and the Templars in due course went on their way, while Richard and his companions rode as fast as they could towards the Hungarian border.

This remote land was friendly territory, for Margaret of France, the widow of Henry the Young King, had married the King of Hungary, and friendly diplomatic relations between Hungary and the Plantagenets had continued thereafter. No doubt when Richard landed on the Adriatic coast he intended to make first for Hungary, and then journey in a north-westerly curve through the lands of his brother-in-law, Henry the Lion, Duke of Saxony, avoiding the territories of the Holy Roman Emperor, Henry VI of Hohenstaufen.

The Holy Roman emperors, whose domains were rougly coterminous with what is now Germany, claimed to be the heirs of the empire of Charlemagne, who in the year 800 had been crowned by the pope as the first 'Holy' Roman Emperor, the Christian heir and reviver of the fallen empire of Rome.

Through this attenuated connection with ancient grandeur and authority, the German Holy Roman emperors claimed suzerainty over all other Christian rulers except the Greek emperors, a secular parallel to the spiritual authority claimed by the Papacy. Reluctant lip-service to this idea was accompanied by political resistance to it. The kings of France also thought themselves the heirs of Charlemagne, which they could do without contradiction, since his empire had included a large proportion of Western Christendom.

Richard I's position in relation to the Holy Roman Empire was unforunate. His brother-in-law Henry the Lion was a consistent opponent of the Hohenstaufens, and Richard himself, while in Sicily, had reached an agreement with Tancred of Lecce to resist imperial claims to the island. Therefore, as Richard journeyed home with two companions, he was as anxious to avoid the lands of Henry of Hohenstaufen as those of Leopold of Austria.

On 28 December 1192, the Emperor Henry VI wrote to Philip Augustus of France:

> We have deemed it proper to inform Your Nobleness, by means of these present letters, that while the enemy of our Empire and the disturber of your Kingdom, Richard, King of England, was sailing homewards to his dominions it chanced that the winds caused him to be shipwrecked . . . and . . . our dearly beloved Cousin, Leopold, Duke of Austria, laid hold of the aforesaid King, in a humble village household near Vienna.

Richard's capture, some eight days previously, had resulted from his complete inability to be self-effacing. He had found lodgings in the household the emperor described, and sent out the German-speaking youth to buy food, providing him with a gold *besant*, a high-denomination Byzantine coin. Great excitement was aroused in the Austrian village market by the sight of a foreign coin representing a very large sum of money. Then everyone wanted to see the rich merchant who had sent his servant shopping with so much wealth. The youth beat a hasty retreat from such dangerous curiosity. However, the travellers were very hungry, so he was sent out again a little later, probably with a handful of less obtrusive coins. But it was bitterly cold, and Richard lent his servant his gloves. They were embroidered with the golden leopards of Anjou, which conclusively revealed his identity.

Trapped at last, by the results of his thoughtlessness, Richard insisted on surrendering to none but Leopold of Austria. The duke was duly brought to receive his sword, and Richard entered captivity with as much appearance of courageous confidence as if he were going to war.

Leopold handed over his prisoner to his suzerain the emperor, with the agreement that Leopold should receive a proportion of the ransom eventually secured for him. Richard was the most valuable prisoner who could have fallen into the emperor's hands. If the English wanted their king back they would have to bid higher than Philip Augustus, who might pay very highly indeed to keep him, or have him kept, a prisoner. The emperor needed all the money he could gather to resist Henry the Lion, to quell a rebellion of German princes in the lower Rhineland, and to fulfil his ambition of conquering Siciliy. He resolved to auction his captive, and in the meantime he kept his place of imprisonment secret.

However, Richard's subjects were soon making efforts to find him. Somehow, Walter of Coutances, Archbishop of Rouen, acquired a copy of the emperor's letter to the King of France, which he displayed before a meeting of the Great Council of the Realm of England on 28 February 1193. It was immediately resolved that the abbots of Boxley and Robertsbridge should travel to Germany to seek the king. They found him at Ochsenfurt near Würtzburg, where he was staying on a journey from his first place of imprisonment, Dürnstein, on the Danube, to Speyer, where he was to meet the emperor.

That is the true story of how King Richard was found: by two official emissaries from England. More familiar is the legend of how the troubadour Blondel wandered from one German castle to another, singing beneath barred windows, until he heard King Richard's voice respond with the next verse of his song. This famous story was first told by a poet known as the Minstrel of Rheims in the following century. Yet there was a knight and troubadour named John de Nesles, who was nicknamed Blondel because of his fair good looks. It was not impossible that he joined the search for Richard, although it was the two abbots who found him.

News of King Richard's capture and imprisonment caused a deep sense of outrage throughout Christendom, because Crusaders, and the lands of absent Crusaders, were supposed to enjoy immunity from any form of molestation, under a general agreement known as the Truce of God. It was usually observed because everyone's interests were best served by keeping it. The case of King Richard was the most outstanding exception to prove the rule.

The first public appearance of Richard after his capture was at the conference at Speyer, which was held on 21 and 22 March 1193. Richard was required to answer the emperor's accusations that he had conspired against the Holy Roman Empire with Henry the Lion and Tancred of Lecce, that he had insulted Leopold of Austria and that he had been a party to the murder of Conrad of Montferrat.

It was reported that Richard's answering speech was so eloquent that it moved his hearers to tears, and so convincing that it caused the emperor spontaneously to rise and give him the Kiss of Peace. This theatrical gesture no doubt symbolized that Richard was not to be regarded as a blame worthy captive, but an ordinary ransomable prisoner of war. Philip Augustus' chances of keeping his enemy mouldering in a dungeon were diminishing.

Fortunately for Richard, the conference at Speyer was attended by one of his most loyal supporters, Hubert Walter, Bishop of Salisbury, who had been with him in the Holy Land, and was travelling homewards through Italy when he heard the news of his king's imprisonment. He broke his journey at Rome to request the support of Pope Celestine III in securing the King of England's liberation, and then he set off for Speyer.

Hubert Walter was a man in whom Richard had the utmost confidence. Richard sent him back to England with a letter requesting Queen Eleanor to secure his appointment as Archbishop of Canterbury, for Archbishop Baldwin had died in the Holy Land.

By May Hubert Walter's appointment was duly secured, and later in the year he was also appointed justiciar. Before the end of 1193 he was the most powerful man in England, and he employed his power more tactfully than William de Longchamp had done. It has been neatly observed that he 'did for Richard what Richard's father had hoped that Thomas Becket would do for him'.

Eleanor of Aquitaine, who supported Hubert Walter as her son requested, had not been idle. While Hubert Walter had visited the pope, Eleanor had written to him, furiously signing herself 'Eleanor, by the wrath of God, Queen of England', and upbraiding him in bitter terms for having done nothing at all to assist Richard's release. In fact, Celestine III had excommunicated Leopold of Austria for breaking the Truce of God and laying hands on a Crusader, but he hesitated to excommunicate the emperor.

No doubt Hubert Walter and the two abbots, who returned to England together, were able to reassure Eleanor that her son would be liberated; it remained to negotiate and to collect the ransom. The result of the negotiations was communicated by William de Longchamp, Richard's next important visitor, who informed the government of England that the emperor would require a hundred and fifty thousand marks to release his captive. This sum of money represented thirty-five tons of silver!

A special government department was set up to collect the ransom, the *Scaccarium Redemptionis* (Exchequer of Ransom), separate from the permanent exchequer. The collection was entrusted to a committee of which the members were two ecclesiastics, Hubert Walter and Richard, Bishop of London; two barons, William, Earl of Arundel and Hamelin, Earl of Warenne, and one burgess, Henry FitzAylwin, Mayor of London. The inclusion of the last is indicative of the prosperity of London at this period, and of the growing influence of the merchant class which he represented.

Beneath the avid eyes of Eleanor of Aquitaine, and the careful accounting of the committee, thirty-five tons of silver began to accumulate, stored in the crypt of St Paul's. Perhaps the collection of it gave rise to the proverbial expression 'a King's Ransom' to describe any vast sum.

Every freeman in the land – that is everyone who was not a 'serf' or un-free agricultural labourer – had to contribute a quarter of his annual income and of the value of his possessions. This was a heavy demand, yet the popularity of the hero of Christendom survived it. Churches were required to contribute their altar plate, though some richer foundations preferred to pay the equivalent value in ready money and keep their sacred vessels, which were often magnificent works of art. The austere Cistercian order which possessed no church ornaments contributed a year's revenue from the sale of the wool yielded by the order's vast flocks of sheep.

While the ransom was collected Richard fretted his time away in prison, drinking his gaolers under the table, and writing verses which speak eloquently for any prisoner in any age:

> No prisoner can tell his honest thought
> Unless he speaks as one who suffers wrong;
> But for his comfort he may make a song.
> My friends are many, but their gifts are naught.
> Shame will be theirs, if, for my ransom, here
>   I lie another year . . .
> The ancient proverb now I know for sure:
> Death and a prison know nor kind nor tie,
> Since for mere lack of gold they let me lie
> Much for myself I grieve; for them still more.
> After my death they will have grievous wrong
>   If I am prisoner long.
> What marvel that my heart is sad and sore
> When my own lord torments my helpless lands!
> Well do I know that, if he held his hands,
> Remembering the common oath we swore,
> I should not here imprisoned with my song
>   Remain a prisoner long . . .

The pyramid of thirty-five tons of silver was slowly built, but in the meantime Richard's enemies were as eager to keep him imprisoned as his friends were to secure his liberation.

Philip Augustus, of whom Richard had written 'my own lord torments my helpless lands', cared nothing for the Truce of God. Neither did Prince John.

Early in 1193 John went to France and paid homage to Philip Augustus for all Richard's continental domains (and according to rumour for England as well) and promised to marry Alys of France. He then returned to England to attempt to overthrow the government, which remained loyal to Richard.

Despite the strong position in England which Richard's generosity had given him, John was conspicuously unsuccessful. He looked for support from Wales and Scotland, but though he was able to hire Welsh mercenaries he received from Wales no voluntary help. The Scots refused to aid him either for love or money.

William the Lion, King of Scots, who had joined the rebellion of Henry the Young King against Henry II, after his capture at Alnwick had been obliged to do homage to Henry II for his own kingdom of Scotland, as the price of his release. When Richard I had been raising money for the Third Crusade, William had re-purchased the full sovereignty of Scotland for a payment of ten thousand marks. He would not risk his recovered independence in the interests of John's ambition.

Richard's situation proved similar to William's, for before his release he was obliged to pay homage to the Emperor Henry VI, and to acknowledge England a fief of the Holy Roman Empire. It is unlikely that either the King of Scots or the King of England took seriously an act of homage performed under duress; but any king who found himself in such a situation made haste to extricate himself, if only for reasons of prestige, and hesitated to risk a repetition of it.

Philip Augustus, relying upon his intrigues with the emperor to keep Richard out of the way for some time to come, invaded Normandy. Gilbert Vascoeuil, the commander of the key fortress of Gisors, surrendered it to him, and Philip overran the long-contested Vexin. He approached Rouen, which was successfully defended by the Earl of Leicester.

Richard, while he remained captive, had steadily improved his relations with the Emperor. He managed to prevent a projected meeting between the Emperor and Philip Augustus in the summer of 1193; he negotiated a settlement between the Emperor and the rebellious Rhineland princes; he also promised to reconcile the Emperor with Henry the Lion of Saxony, and if he failed, to pay a further instalment of ransom.

Philip realised that it would be prudent to make a truce with Richard, who would obviously gain his release before long; so, in July 1193, he concluded the Treaty of Mantes, in which Richard – who, after all, was not yet in a position to offer much resistance – agreed that Philip should keep his gains. But Philip knew what the future held in store: he sent John the famous message 'Look to yourself, the Devil is loosed.' John precipitately abandoned his efforts to take over the government of England, and fled to the French court.

The French king was still planning ahead. If he could not overthrow the King of England with the concurrence of the emperor, he would turn to untried allies. He made an alliance with Cnut VI, King of Denmark, who was to provide him with a fleet for the invasion of England. On 15 August 1193 he married Cnut's daughter, Ingeborg of Denmark, and the following day he repudiated her and endeavoured to return her to the Danish ambassadors who had brought her to France. They refused to take her, and departed at once, leaving Ingeborg as an unwanted Queen of France. Philip Augustus was prepared to sacrifice his alliance with Denmark and to defy papal condemnation of his behaviour, but nothing would induce him to cohabit with Ingeborg of Denmark. The story invites the attention of the historical novelist, for it leaves the historian without even the materials of conjecture.

Whatever the cause of Philip's repudiation of Ingeborg, it was greatly to Richard's advantage. Philip and John were reduced to a direct attempt to bribe the emperor to continue Richard's captivity, but such an arrangement could only be temporary, and the emperor found the offer less interesting in view of Richard's useful diplomatic influence. He had, as a recompense for Richard's efforts, offered to make him King of Provence – though in fact he lacked the authority over that region to do more than bestow on Richard a title for which he would have to fight. Richard was attracted by the idea of another kingdom, but in his scale of priorities the recovery of the lost Vexin took first place.

Eleanor of Aquitaine brought the king's ransom to Germany early in 1194.

On 2 February, the feast of Candlemas, Richard and Eleanor met for the first time since Eleanor had brought Berengaria of Navarre to Messina. Eleanor doubtless bore the marks of increased age, and Richard those of captivity; but no alteration of appearances could mar the joy of their reunion. Mother and son began a triumphal journey home, voyaging down the Rhine, to be received with honour wherever they stepped ashore.

Richard was back in England on 12 March. He landed at Sandwich, and then rode to Canterbury, to give thanks for his safe return at the shrine of St Thomas Becket. When he rode into London on 23 March, Queen Eleanor rode at his side. The populace cheered itself hoarse with enthusiasm for the king and his mother. For Queen Berengaria, self-effacing or ruthlessly effaced, apparently nobody spared a thought.

IV
The Passing of Coeur de Lion

Ai! Seigner Dieus! Vos q'etz perdonaire
Vers Dieus, vers hom, vera vida, merces!
Perdonatz li, que ops e concha l'es,
e no gardetz, Seigner, al sieu faillir
e membre vos cum vos anet servir.

(O Lord God, Thou who art all-merciful,
True God, true Man, true Life, be pitiful,
And pardon him who has of pardon need,
And to his sins, O Lord, pay Thou no heed,
But how he would have served Thee, be mindful.)

(Gaucelem Faidit, on the death of Richard I)

On 17 April 1194 King Richard knelt at the feet of Hubert Walter, in the priory church of St Swithin at Winchester, and for a second time received the crown of England.

The rite was so majestically solemn that it has been called a second coronation, but in all probability it was intended to be a spectacle and not a sacrament. Richard had been crowned and anointed in 1189, and neither imprisonment nor homage to the emperor made necessary a renewal of his consecration, as some writers have suggested. But the kings of England had been accustomed to appear before their subjects at solemn 'Crown Wearings' two or three times a year, on major feasts of the Church. Richard had not worn his crown in England since his coronation, so it was not surprising if some who witnessed the Crown Wearing at Winchester thought that he was being crowned anew.

Queen Eleanor, for whom a special dais had been built, presided over the scene from her exalted place. Queen Berengaria was conspicuous only by her absence. After Richard's fleet had been scattered on the homeward voyage, Berengaria and Joanna had travelled through Italy together, and stayed for a time in Rome. Richard had not seen his queen since they were in the Holy Land, and he seemed in no haste to do so.

In 1195 Richard was admonished by a hermit, who urged him to remember the destruction of Sodom, and to turn away from unlawful pleasures. Richard repented his sins with all the extravagance which he had displayed at Messina, and sent for his neglected wife. But he had married her for the sake of duty, and he was reunited with her in a spirit of repentance; neither state of mind provided a basis for a successful marriage, and neither led to the begetting of an heir.

The month after the Crown Wearing Richard left England for the last time. He went to join battle with Philip Augustus, and his campaigns to restore the Angevin Empire to its utmost limits occupied the rest of his life.

It was said that from the time he left the Holy Land to the time that he received the Last Sacrament on his deathbed, Richard refused to take Holy Communion because of the hatred which he bore to the King of France. Probably he hated him with the special virulence which people reserve for hating those whom they have once loved.

Richard's initial attack was so successful that Prince John decided his wisest course would be to abandon Philip and throw himself on his brother's mercy. He came to Richard at Lisieux, fell at his feet, and asked pardon for his multitudinous treacheries. John evidently knew his brother as well as his brother knew him. Richard's affection for John was ready and contemptuous.

'Do not be afraid, John,' he said, 'You are a child. You have been in bad company, and it is those who have led you astray who will be punished.'

He commanded that a fine salmon, which had just been presented to him by some citizens of Lisieux, should be cooked to feast his brother.

John was twenty-seven in 1194, scarcely a child any longer, but Richard's words of forgiveness suggest that the impression he created was still one of tiresomeness rather than of serious evil-doing. However, from 1194 onwards John began to be a man to be taken seriously. He consistently supported Richard against Philip Augustus, though probably less from motives of gratitude than from the conclusion that he had joined the winning side.

However, fighting Philip Augustus was rather like doing battle with the elements: he might retreat like the tide, but like the tide he always came back. It was a notorious fact that he feared to meet Richard in pitched battle, yet in siege operations, in surprise attacks, in swift marches to the relief of some beleaguered fortress, his generalship matched Richard's. He won no admiration as a soldier because he was personally cautious to the point of cowardice; but Richard was probably aware that he was opposing a strategist of equal resource.

From Lisieux Richard marched roughly south, to chase Philip Augustus out of Verneuil. He then advanced southward into Touraine and by the middle of June he had recaptured the great stronghold of Loches, which he had been forced to cede to Philip during his captivity. He then turned sharply north again, for Philip, defeated in one place, had attacked in another.

It was at Fréteval, long ago the scene of the hollow reconciliation of Henry II and Thomas Becket, that Richard inflicted upon Philip Augustus his most humiliating defeat. On 4 July 1194, while Philip hid – or took sanctuary – in a church, Richard's army seized his camp and captured arms and horses, siege machines and supplies, documents (which were invaluable for intelligence purposes), and cartloads of ready money.

William Marshal, now an ageing warrior, had been in command of the reserves that day, and their services had not been required. Richard reminded some young knights, who were inclined to boast of their achievements, of an important lesson in warfare:

'The Marshal did better than any of you,' he observed, 'if there had been any trouble he would have helped us. When one has a good reserve, one does not fear one's enemies.'

In fact, William Marshal had probably resented his inability to get to grips with the enemy, for a year or two later he performed a notable feat of arms which won the admiration and also aroused the concern of King Richard.

One day, when Richard was besieging the castle of Milli, near Beauvais, one of his knights named Guy de La Bruyère ascended a scaling ladder, whereupon one of the defenders caught him round the neck with a huge fork like a pitchfork, and held him helpless. William Marshal, seeing what had happened, rushed up the scaling ladder and fought so fiercely that he not only rescued La Bruyère but gained possession of a long section of the wall. William's men-at-arms, shouting 'The castle is taken! To his aid! To his aid!' followed him up the ladder, just in time to see William Marshal fell the Constable of Milli with a mighty blow and then sit down on his unconscious body to gasp for breath and take stock of the situation. The castle was soon surrendered.

When Richard arrived he said to William Marshal:

'Sir Marshal, it is not fitting for a man of your rank and prowess to risk yourself in such feats. Leave them to young knights who must win renown. As for your captive, were he a hundred times more valuable, I would give him to you.'

Richard was no doubt anxious to preserve the life of a valued servant, and a man for whom he felt respect and affection; but it is amusing to hear him discouraging an older man from performing just such deeds of daring as he himself would have continued to perform, had he lived so long.

The fighting was halted towards the end of July 1194 by a truce, and the next year a serious attempt was made to negotiate a peace. But the Treaty of Louviers of 1195 was doomed to become a dead letter, for its terms satisfied the ambitions neither of Richard nor of Philip Augustus. Richard was still deprived of the Vexin, and Philip had lost Issodoun and Graçay, in Berri. Each was determined to recover the territory ceded to the other.

Richard offered the first provocation when he began to build a mighty castle on the rock of Les Andelys, high above a bend of the river Seine, dominating the landscape and threatening the domains of the King of France. This great fortress was Château Gaillard – the 'Saucy Castle' – which one authoritative writer on this period has called 'the most famous castle of the Middle Ages'. Richard designed it with all the skill which he had attained through his experience of siege and defence during years of warfare in Aquitaine, Sicily, Cyprus, Palestine and the contested borders of the Angevin Empire. He built it to threaten his adversary, yet should his adversary turn the tables on him, he believed that it would prove impregnable.

Château Gaillard was swiftly built; no time was wasted in carving ornamentation. The beauty of the building was that of perfect relationship to its site, and of perfect adaptation to its function. Richard was completely satisfied with what he had built. 'How fair is this year-old daughter of mine!' he is said to have exclaimed when he saw his castle completed.

Richard's jesting reference to his castle as his child may reveal a deep-seated anxiety about his lack of heirs. There is indeed a story by a contemporary writer, Gerald the Welshman, that Richard once complained to a priest of his failure to beget children. The priest had the temerity to reply:

'You have three daughters, Sire – Pride, Covetousness and Lechery.'

Richard did not take offence, but with a great gust of laughter he called a group of knights within hearing, and said:

'I am told by this priest here that I have three daughters, and I desire you to witness of how I would have them bestowed: my daughter Pride, to the Templars and Hospitallers; my daughter Covetousness, upon the members of the Cistercian order; and my daughter Lechery, upon the clergy.'

The story is probably untrue, for it is almost too neatly artificial to be convincing. But if it is true, it reveals in Richard a quick wit, a streak of anti-clericalism, and a short memory for the generosity with which the Cistercian order had helped to ransom him.

Richard's fair daughter Château Gaillard was a cause of contention from the outset. Richard had chosen his site for military reasons, and it did not trouble him that Les Andelys was a possession of the archbishops of Rouen. Even the loyal Walter of Coutances felt obliged to make a vigorous protest against the king's invasion of his archbishopric. Richard arranged an exchange of lands which was financially greatly to Walter of Coutances' advantage; but Richard cared for nothing but his determination that no consideration upon earth should interfere with the construction of his castle. 'He took such pleasure in the building,' wrote William of Newburgh, 'that, if I am not mistaken, if an angel had descended from Heaven and told him to abandon it, that angel would have been met with a volley of curses and the work would have gone on regardless.'

While Richard was building Château Gaillard, he was also constructing a network of alliances for the discomfiture of Philip Augustus.

By now it was Richard and not Philip who was the ally of the emperor. In July 1195 the emperor had sent Richard a crown, and commanded him as a vassal of the Holy Roman Empire to invade the dominions of the French king, and not to make peace with him without imperial consent. He remitted the last seventeen thousand marks of Richard's ransom, to help him finance his war.

Henry the Lion of Saxony died in 1195, leaving two sons, Henry and Otto, both of whom were on good terms with their uncle King Richard. Henry married the daughter of the Count Palatine of the Rhine, and became Count Palatine in right of his wife in the same year. In 1196 Richard created Otto Count of Poitou, and for the next two years kept the young man with him on his campaigns. Richard had never come to a final decision as to whether his brother John or his nephew Arthur of Brittany should be nominated as his heir. Perhaps he was contemplating a third candidate in his other nephew, Otto. However, in 1197 the Emperor Henry VI died. The imperial crown was elective, and Richard's influence among the princes of Germany enabled him to secure the election of Otto as 'King of the Romans', or emperor designate. With the son of a Plantagenet mother in control of the empire, the situation of Philip Augustus was beginning to look black.

It worsened still further when Innocent III, one of the most powerful popes of the Middle Ages, ascended the papal throne in 1198. Innocent took up the cause of Philip's repudiated queen, Ingeborg of Denmark, and placed Philip's kingdom under an Interdict.

By 1198 Philip had arrayed against him the might of the Holy Roman Empire, the Angevin Empire and the Papacy. He had lesser enemies also, among them Richard's brother-in-law King Sancho VII of Navarre, and Raymond VI, Count of Toulouse, whom Joanna had consented to wed in 1196. Perhaps she would have done better to have married Saphadin, for Raymond VI, like his father, proved to be a pattern of treachery, and a cruel and unfaithful husband.

In September 1198, Philip Augustus endured a crushing defeat at Courcelles-lès-Gisors, one of the castles of the contested Vexin, which he was attempting to relieve. Richard, with a force of mercenaries led by a famous captain named Mercadier, fell upon the French and drove them in headlong flight towards the great fortress of Gisors itself. The bridge over the river Epte at the gate of Gisors collapsed under the press of fleeing knights, and King Philip himself suffered the indignity of falling into the river.

Richard proudly reported his success to the Bishop of Durham:

'Thus have we defeated the King of France at Gisors; but it is not we who have done the same, but rather God and our right (*Dieu et mon droit*), by our means . . .'

It is believed that this letter was the origin of the use of the words '*Dieu et mon Droit*' as the motto of the English royal house.

Richard's position, however, was not as strong as it appeared to be. He was in desperate financial straits. He had bled his domains white, collecting money first for his Crusade, then for his ransom, then for his wars with Philip Augustus, the cost of which had included the hiring of mercenaries and building of Château Gaillard.

In 1196 Hubert Walter claimed that in the past two years England had provided Richard with 1,100,000 marks. If it is remembered that 150,000 marks represented 35 tons of silver, the scale of extortion which this brilliant administrator had achieved on behalf of his king can begin to be imagined. Richard was coming to the end of his resources; he might win battles, but he needed peace.

Philip Augustus was equally in need of peace. Hubert Walter, who was sent to the French court to negotiate, arranged a truce to last till St Hilary's Day, 13 January 1199. On that day Richard and Philip Augustus met for the last time, though they were too inimical to approach each other. Not far from Château Gaillard, Richard sat in a boat on the Seine and Philip Augustus sat on his horse on the river bank, while a papal legate, Peter of Capua, negotiated the peace terms. The agreement was simple: peace should be kept for five years, each king holding what he possessed at present.

The treaty offered a breathing space, rather than a long-term solution.

Early in the spring of 1199 a peasant was ploughing in a field beside Chaluz, near Limoges. He turned up a wonderful treasure, which was described as 'An Emperor, with his wife and daughters, all of gold and seated at a round golden table'; there was also a hoard of ancient coins. The peasant took the treasure, which was probably Roman, to his lord, Archard of Chaluz, who in turn sent some of the treasure to his own lord, Aimar of Limoges, who loyally sent it on to King Richard.

Richard thought that what he had received was not comparable with the richness of the original finds as they had been described to him. He guessed that Archard of Chaluz was trying to keep most of the treasure for himself. Need, greed and his rights as suzerain probably all contributed to Richard's decision to attack the castle of Chaluz and seize the treasure for himself.

On the evening of 26 March Richard, with the bold Mercadier by his side, was reconnoitering. Together they walked slowly round the castle, studying its defences. High on the ramparts stood a young archer, armed with a crossbow. Deliberately he took his aim, and the short bolt from his bow hit King Richard in the shoulder.

Richard ran back to his lodging in the village of Chaluz. The wound, though painful, did not seem serious. He tried to pull out the bolt for himself, and it snapped off, leaving the barbed head embedded in his shoulder.

Mercadier sent for his surgeon to cut it out. A mercenary captain who was called 'The Prince of the Routiers' would doubtless have had an excellent surgeon in his employ, but not all the skill of Salerno could avail if a wound became infected. Although the head of the crossbow-bolt was successfully cut from Richard's shoulder, an infection set in and a few days later the king knew that he was dying.

He made his confession, received the Last Sacrament, and with characteristically passionate repentance declared that to expiate his sins he was ready to remain in Purgatory until the Last Judgment. He sent the Abbot of Turpenay to bring Queen Eleanor, who was staying at Fontevrault Abbey, to be with him at his death.

While Richard lay on his deathbed, Mercadier pressed on with the siege of the castle of Chaluz, stormed it, and butchered the garrison to a man, preserving only the crossbowman, whom he brought before King Richard.

Richard said to him:

'What harm have I done you that you have killed me?'

The young man, who felt that he himself was facing imminent death, answered bravely:

'You slew my father and my two brothers with your own hand, and you had meant to kill me. Therefore take what revenge on me you may think fit, for I will readily endure the greatest tortures you can devise, so long as you have met your end after having inflicted so many and so great evils upon the world.'

Richard was facing not merely death but the judgment of God; with that in mind he said:

'I forgive you my death. You may go free.'

The young man went out, but Mercadier who had a great regard for King Richard was not going to see the man who had killed him go unpunished. Nor would he disobey Richard by killing the man himself. He sent him to the unhappy Joanna of Toulouse, who showed her love for her brother by having his killer blinded, flayed alive, and torn apart by horses. A few months later she left her husband, took the veil at Fontevrault, and died there. She had shown herself as savagely cruel and as passionately repentant as any of the men of her family.

Richard died in the arms of Queen Eleanor on 6 April 1199. She had his body carried to Fontevrault, where it was buried on 11 April after St Hugh of Avalon, Bishop of Lincoln, had celebrated the Mass of the Dead. On his way to the king's funeral St Hugh had visited Queen Berengaria at Beaufort-en-Vallée, to tell her of her husband's death. Richard had sent her no message and left her no bequest; but despite his neglect he had inspired her love, and she grieved for him profoundly.

In his continental lands, which had suffered so from the depredations of warfare, Richard was not mourned. Someone wrote a savage epitaph for him:

Virus, avaritia, scelus, enormisque libido,
Faeda fames, atrox elatio, caeca cupido,
Annis regnarunt bis quinis; arcabalista
Arte, manu, telo, prostravit viribus ista.
(Venom, avarice, crime, unbridled lust,
Foul famine, atrocious pride and blinded greed
A decade reigned. An archer did this deed –
His hand, skill, weapon, strength, brought all to dust.)

The troubadour Gaucelem Faidit, whose lament was quoted at the beginning of this chapter, thought more charitably of his king.

It remained for the English to make a hero of Richard Coeur de Lion: to invent stories of his friendship with the outlaw Robin Hood, to explain his nickname not by the simple fact that he was lion-hearted in his courage, but by the strange tale that he had once wrestled with a lion and torn the heart out of the beast's body. It was also told in a later romance that he had not been the son of Queen Eleanor but of a demon mother named Cassodorien, of whom the same story was told as of his legendary ancestress Melusine.

Richard was a flawed hero, yet he possessed heroic qualities which appealed to successive generations of Englishmen. He spent approximately six months of a ten years' reign in England, and his only gifts to his English subjects were the insubstantial materials of his legend, and the realities of extortion upon extortion. That Richard the feckless hero was popular, and that his father the dedicated ruler was unpopular, may indicate the collective stupidity of mankind, or it may indicate the importance of food for the imagination, the profound truth that 'Man doth not live by bread only . . .'

Surroundings

Medieval landscape. The countryside ceaselessly alters as men discover different ways of exploiting their environment. Medieval agriculture gave the land a very different appearance from that of modern farming. The aerial photograph shows the medieval 'open field' system still in use at Laxton in Nottinghamshire as an example. The unfenced fields were divided into strips and the 'villein', or un-free tenant, farmed a holding composed of scattered strips, the intention being to ensure a fair distribution of land of varying quality (AEROFILMS)

Aerial view of the remains of the medieval town of Salisbury, now known as Old Sarum. The medieval town occupied the site of the Roman Sorviodunum, and of an earlier Iron-Age encampment. The oldest fortifications, the Norman castle and the cruciform foundations of the early cathedral can be seen (AEROFILMS)

Medieval towns were dominated by secular and religious symbols of power: castles and churches. Dover Castle, rebuilt much in its present form by Henry II, dominated Dover and protected the most vulnerable part of the English coast (DEPARTMENT OF THE ENVIRONMENT, CROWN COPYRIGHT)

The Chapel of Dover Castle. Despite religio-political power struggles, Church was the soul of the State in the twelfth century, and every seat of secular power contained its chapel (DEPARTMENT OF THE ENVIRONMENT, CROWN COPYRIGHT)

An impressive image of the Church dominant: the Cathedral of Le Mans, in which Count Geoffrey Plantagenet was buried. The city was the birthplace of Henry II, and its burning in 1189 was a mortal blow to an already defeated and dying king (N. D. ROGER-VIOLLET)

The austere interior of the Abbey of Fontevrault, in which Henry II, Eleanor of Aquitaine, Richard Coeur-de-Lion, and other members of the Plantagenet family are buried (JEAN ROUBIER)

A domestic insight: the exterior and interior of the kitchen of the Abbey of Fontevrault (JEAN ROUBIER)

The Castle of Chinon, in which Henry II died (JEAN ROUBIER)

The 'Tour du Moulin' at Chinon, a picture which gives a vivid impression of the dominating presence of such a castle, and of the mastery of the locality which possession of such a building conferred on its commander (JEAN ROUBIER)

Dürnstein on the Danube, one of the castles in which Richard Coeur de Lion was imprisoned after his capture by Leopold of Austria, on his homeward journey from the Third Crusade (ARCHIV FÜR KUNST UND GESCHICHTE)

Château Gaillard, the 'Saucy Castle' which Richard Coeur de Lion built on the rock of Les Andelys, a commanding position above the river Seine, to protect his lands against the ambitions of Philip Augustus of France (JEAN ROUBIER)

The ruins of Corfe Castle, Dorset, in which King John was rumoured to have starved to death twenty-two of the prisoners captured at Mirebeau in 1202 (A.F. KERSTING)

Newark Castle, the scene of King John's death in 1216 (A. F. KERSTING)

PART THREE
King John

John . . . *Remember what was said of the brave and scholarly King Alfred—that at the end of his reign it was possible for a man to hang golden drinking cups beside a simple wayside fountain, and to have no fear that they would be stolen—or even borrowed. If I in my due time could be laid in a tomb with that epitaph graven over it, I could then regard myself as a fit successor to my famous father. As for my no less famous mother, her beautiful, stubborn and deceitful spirit has so wound itself into my uncomely body, that not only does my right hand not know what my left hand is doing—which is indeed recommended in the Holy Gospel—but actual bloody conflict between these two unhappy members prevails every day of my life . . .*
(John Arden, *Left-Handed Liberty,* Act II, Scene IV)

I

The Legacy of a Legend

Queen
When I was but twelve years old
I was betrothed to a lord of France:
But the wild King of England grinned
over the garden wall
Where I and my little maidens did dance.
John
She was as beautiful and delicate a child
As ever I had seen.
And upon that sunlit afternoon
I determined she would be my Queen . . .
It has been alleged
In terms of political scandal
That we took so long time in our tent
On a morning to kiss and fondle
That the battle was lost and broken
And Saucy Castle taken
And yet no man could stir me to rise.
It was more than a scandal
It was in fact a pack of lies.

(John Arden, *Left-Handed Liberty*, Act II, Scene IV)

William Marshal brought the news of King Richard's death to Hubert Walter. Both men were in Normandy at the time, and late at night on 10 April 1199, William knocked up the archbishop who was retiring to bed in his lodging at Vaudreuil. Both of them recognized the need to prevent the troubles attendant upon a disputed succession.

'My lord,' said William Marshal, 'we must lose no time in choosing some-one to be king.'

'I think', replied Hubert Walter, 'that Arthur should rightfully be king.'

William Marshal held the opposing view.

'To my mind that would be bad,' he said, 'Arthur is counselled by traitors; he is haughty and proud; and if we put him over us he will only do us harm for he does not love the people of this land [they were speaking of England] . . . Consider rather Count John: he seems to me the nearer heir to the land which belonged to his father and brother.'

'Marshal,' demanded Hubert Walter, 'is this really your desire?'

'Yes, my lord, for it is just,' William answered, 'undoubtedly a son has a better claim to his father's land than a grandson; it is right that he should have it.'

'So be it, then,' said Hubert Walter, 'but mark my words, Marshal, you will never regret anything in your life as much as this.'

King John's accession was thus assured by the agreement of two of the most influential among the many ecclesiastics and lay magnates who had served his brother. But it was small wonder that Hubert Walter had his reservations, for John was perhaps the most erratic character produced by a family of violently inconsistent personalities.

As the last child of parents who were estranged soon after his birth, John was brought up in an emotional no-man's-land. He must have been a stranger to his mother, though he was the favourite of his often-absent father. That Henry II nicknamed him John 'Sans Terre' probably implanted in his mind the idea that he was a prince without possessions and without prospects.

While he was a small boy John lived at Fontevrault as an oblate, a child destined for the religious life. He reacted violently against it. There was no question that he would submit to a vocation of convenience, like his bastard brother Geoffrey Plantagenet, Archbishop of York. The Church, even as the path of advancement, was not acceptable to John. His experience of Fontevrault made him that rarity in the medieval world, an irreligious man. In later life his daily obligation to participate in religious ritual was so irksome to him that once, at the conclusion of a stag hunt he addressed himself to the dead buck with the words 'You happy beast – never forced to patter prayers nor dragged to the Sacrament!'

There is some truth in two lines of A. A. Milne's famous children's poem:

King John was not a good man,
And no good friends had he . . .

This was not altogether surprising, because since he had betrayed his father, his brother and Philip Augustus, no one regarded him as trustworthy; in consequence, he was unable to risk trusting anyone else. He would demand oaths and hostages from barons who were insulted by the suggestion that they would have been false to their suzerain; he was obliged to depend upon the services of mercenary captains, such as Savary de Mauléon, Gerard d'Athée and Faulkes de Bréauté, whose loyalty was purchased.

Yet his faults were balanced by his qualities. After he had been removed from Fontevrault, he was brought up in the household of the Justiciar

Ranulf Glanville. John responded to his influence far better than his eldest brother the Young King had responded to the influence of Thomas Becket, or of William Marshal. John developed a real interest in administration and a genuine concern for justice. Though he might betray a fellow sovereign and distrust a powerful baron, his concern for the welfare of his ordinary subjects resembled that of his father. Humble litigants, whose cases King John indefatigably travelled England to hear, had a far better chance of receiving good justice from him than from Richard Coeur de Lion.

John was criticized for being lustful, yet the same charge could have been levelled against Henry II or Richard I. John had a weakness for pretty women, but he treated them with generosity and kindness. When he repudiated his childless wife Havisa of Gloucester (which he was able to do on the grounds of consanguinity) he provided for her generously, and continued to give her presents as the years passed. He was equally generous to Queen Berengaria, whose dowry he repaid. When he had female prisoners or hostages he was usually thoughtful in providing them with necessities and a few luxuries too. John liked women, and – with one appalling exception – he did not exploit his power over them. King John could be genial and generous, or he could be suspicious and sadistic; but certainly he was not the monster of unmitigated wickedness which legend has made him.

Physically John was probably the least impressive member of his family. He stood five feet five inches in height. He was not a short man by the standards of his century, but he was not a kingly figure like his brother Richard. He was red-haired and stockily built, and he put on weight as he grew older. What he lacked in majesty he sought to make good by display; he spent vast sums on rich clothes and loaded himself with jewels. His effigy in Worcester Cathedral, which is thought to be a genuine likeness, shows a face in which cunning, humour and strength of will are forcefully represented.

Despite the efforts of Hubert Walter and William Marshal, King John's accession was not accepted unresistingly throughout the Angevin Empire.

John was acknowledged without trouble by England and Normandy. Eleanor, for whom the death of Richard was probably the supreme anguish of her life, did not allow herself to be paralyzed by it. She toured her duchy, demanded the renewed homage of the barons of Aquitaine, paid her own homage to Philip Augustus, and then invested John as Duke of Aquitaine upon the same terms as Richard had enjoyed that title: that Eleanor should remain Duchess for life. John's mother had shrewdly secured for him a great part of his inheritance.

Anjou, Maine and Touraine, however, preferred to acknowledge Arthur of Brittany. The lords of these lands were probably hoping to take advantage of the opportunities for independent action which would be offered by the suzerainty of an adolescent duke.

Arthur, with the encouragement of his mother Constance – whose lasting hatred of the Plantagenets was probably the legacy of an unhappy marriage – went to Paris and gave his homage to Philip Augustus for all the Plantagenet domains on the continent. Philip Augustus welcomed Arthur, and delightedly resumed his well-established game of setting the Plantagenet lions to fight among themselves; Arthur, far from being a helpless child, was as precociously fierce a youth as any of his uncles had shown themselves to be, when they rebelled against their father.

John, in the meantime, had acted with equal resolution. His first move, on hearing of Richard's death, was to seize the royal treasure, which was in the castle of Chinon; though it might be depleted, clearly it was still worth possessing.

On 25 April 1199 he entered the Norman capital of Rouen, where he was invested with the ducal coronet of golden roses and the ducal lance. There was unseemly merriment from some of John's more frivolous attendants when he dropped the lance; he had the knack of endowing the most solemn occasions with an element of farce. From Normandy he crossed to England where he was crowned in Westminster Abbey on Ascension Day, 27 May. He had secured the heritage of the Norman Kings of England, and his mother was looking after his interests in Aquitaine. Despite the threat of Arthur, his wisest course seemed to be to renew the peace which Richard had made with Philip Augustus.

The terms of the Treaty of Le Goulet, which was concluded the following year, on 22 May 1200, showed that despite the appearance of power created by Richard's victories, as a result of his increasing financial difficulties the long-term advantages had lain with Philip Augustus.

The treaty was reasonable and statesmanlike, though it revealed the realities of the situation. John was to pay Philip twenty thousand marks 'relief', or succession duty, in recognition of his inheritance of the fiefs for which he was Philip's vassal. Philip gained the Vexin, but John kept Château Gaillard and the fortified town on the rock of Les Andelys which had grown up around it. Arthur paid homage to John for the duchy of Brittany. The treaty was sealed, as such treaties frequently were, by a marriage alliance: Philip's son (by his first wife Isabella of Hainault), the Dauphin Louis, was to marry one of John's nieces, a daughter of his sister Eleanor and her husband King Alphonso VIII of Castile. For her dowry the princess was to receive Graçay and Issodoun, which Richard I had captured from Philip.

John had received some gains, in particular the homage of Arthur, in return for his concessions; but some of his more militant barons thought that Richard would not have made any concessions at all. They contemptuously nicknamed John 'King Softsword'; it was easy for them to criticize John, they did not have the ultimate responsibility for financing warfare.

Queen Eleanor recognized the importance of peace as the best means of assisting her youngest son to preserve his inheritance. As her contribution to implementing the Treaty of Le Goulet, Eleanor undertook her last great journey: she herself went to Castile to bring back the Dauphin's bride and to have the happiness of visiting her daughter and namesake, the Queen of Castile. She was a remarkable old lady indeed, who at the age of seventy-eight could ride over the high passes of the Pyrenees with Mercadier and his routiers for her escort. (Mercadier was killed in a brawl on the homeward journey.)

There were three Castilian princesses: Berengaria, Urraca and Blanca. Berengaria was already betrothed to the heir of the Spanish kingdom of Léon, and Urraca had been designated as the bride of the Dauphin. Eleanor of Aquitaine, however, rejected her in favour of Blanca, on the grounds that the French would never accept a queen with the outlandish name of Urraca. (They had, indeed, converted the outlandish name of Ingeborg into the more euphonious 'Isambour'; but, alas, the transformation had not made the Danish queen any more acceptable to her husband.)

Eleanor, having spent the winter at the court of Castile, retraced her journey in the spring of 1201, with the Princess Blanca. On 23 May the marriage of Blanca and Louis took place in Normandy, since France was still under the Interdict of Innocent III. The French called the spanish princess 'Blanche', and Blanche of Castile became a great and formidable Queen of France, and the mother of St Louis. It is not always remembered that St Louis was the great-grandson of Henry II and Eleanor of Aquitaine.

In the summer of 1200 King John made a tour of his continental domains. There seemed to be trouble everywhere, in particular between the counts of Angoulême and the immensely powerful house of Lusignan, which Richard I had done so much to advance. It was alarming, therefore, when a sudden reconciliation took place between these enemies, and they agreed that Isabelle, the daughter of Audemar, Count of Angoulême should marry Hugh IX, known as 'le Brun', Count of Lusignan.

King John was faced with the disagreeable prospect of an alliance between two powerful and turbulent vassals, when, while he was the guest of the Count of Angoulême, he met his entrancing young daughter. At the time, John was negotiating for the hand of a Portuguese princess, so it seems likely that the sight of the irresistible Isabelle of Angoulême affected his susceptible temperament. Political considerations encouraged the promptings of passion: to marry Isabelle would untie the knot of the Lusignan–Angoulême alliance. From Count Audemar's viewpoint the King of England was a far greater match for his daughter than Count Hugh le Brun. The marriage of King John and Isabelle of Angoulême took place on 30 August 1200.

In the insulted Lusignans, John had made powerful enemies; but it was some time before he reaped the consequences of his action. He returned to

England in the autumn of 1200, for the coronation of his queen, and during the summer of 1201 they went together to France, to be entertained sumptuously in Paris, after the wedding of the Dauphin Louis and Blanche of Castile.

John had been casual to the point of provocation in his treatment of the Lusignans. Though he had provided an alternative bride for Count Hugh from among his own royal wards, he had demanded that Hugh's brother Ralph of Lusignan, Count of Eu, should hand over to him the castle of Drincourt in Normandy, to which John had no right at all.

The Lusignans appealed to Philip Augustus, as John's suzerain, for justice, whereupon John seized Drincourt, overran the county of Eu, and proposed that the Lusignans' complaint should be decided by a 'judicial combat' (a battle between the litigants in which the winner was adjudged the legal victor in the dispute). As King John proposed to be represented by professional champions, the Lusignans refused. Philip supported them, and took the opportunity of condemning King John as a 'contumacious vassal', a sentence which implied the forfeiture of his continental fiefs. This situation gave Philip Augustus the perfect excuse to declare war upon John, in order to carry out his sentence.

The war began in the spring of 1202. Philip's intention was to invade and claim Normandy, in which John had acted 'contumaciously', and if the war went well, to 'enfeoff' Arthur with Brittany, Anjou, Maine, Touraine and Poitou, and to rule them as his suzerain.

Arthur set about the conquest of Poitou, aided by the Lusignans. Queen Eleanor, who had been living in retirement at Fontevrault, decided to take refuge in the strong fortress of Mirebeau, north west of Poitiers. Arthur and his allies closed in to besiege her.

King John was mustering his forces at Le Mans, while Hubert Walter was endeavouring to wring a few more tons of silver from the depleted resources of England, when news was brought to John of his mother's plight.

It was 30 July 1202 when John received the news, and it was very early in the morning on 1 August that he forced his way into the town of Mirebeau, through the single gateway which the besiegers of the castle had kept open for the delivery of their supplies.

Eleanor herself was commanding the defence of the castle, and she had positioned archers at every point of vantage. Though she was prepared to die as resolutely as she had lived before she submitted to be captured by her grandson Arthur, Eleanor must have rejoiced that John had bestirred himself so swiftly as to march more than eighty miles in forty-eight hours to save her from death or humiliation.

When John led his mother out of the keep of Mirebeau, the ancient queen must have resembled a mummified relic of her youthful self, yet she had proved triumphantly that age had not quenched the ardour of her spirit.

She returned to Fontevrault to make her peace with God and to pray for her dead. When she herself approached death in the early spring of 1204 she probably felt nearer to her friends and erstwhile enemies in heaven or purgatory than to her two surviving children, Eleanor, Queen of Castile and John, King of England. Reconciled to death, she left the world at the age of eighty-two and left it the poorer for her going.

In the meantime, King John had lost a great part of his inheritance.

At Mirebeau John captured Arthur, the Lusignans, and as he put it 'all our Poitevin enemies'. It was a notable victory, but he nullified it by his treatment of his prisoners. They were loaded with chains and taken to their places of imprisonment in carts: to be forced to ride in a cart was regarded as the ultimate indignity which could be inflicted on a knight. The Lusignans were permitted to ransom themselves, but twenty-two other prisoners were taken to Corfe Castle, and were never heard of again. It was subsequently rumoured that they had been starved to death. John's reputation might have survived these tales of evil doing – as Richard's had survived the well-authenticated reports of his ill-treatment of Isaac Comnenus – had it not been for the stories concerning the fate of Arthur of Brittany.

Arthur was imprisoned first at Falaise and then at Rouen, where it was later reported that King John:

> On the Thursday before Easter [3rd April 1203] when he was drunk and possessed by the Devil . . . slew him with his own hand, and tying a heavy stone to the body cast it into the Seine. It was discovered by a fisherman in his net, and being dragged to the bank and recognized, was taken for secret burial.

The story has been allowed some credibility because it was told to the chronicler of the abbey of Margam in Glamorgan by William de Briouze, a patron of the abbey, who had been the actual captor of Arthur at Mirebeau. It was possible that he may have had inside knowledge of Arthur's subsequent fate wich he passed on to the monk who wrote the chronicle; but the story of Arthur's end rests only upon hearsay evidence, and the personal guilt of King John cannot be regarded as conclusively proved.

However, John had as diabolical a temper as any other member of his family, and Arthur, in William Marshal's words, was 'haughty and proud'. If John, drunk or sober, had decided to visit his prisoner, given the enmity between them, it is easy to imagine a violent scene in which the youth died at the hands of the older and stronger man.

There was another rumour that at Falaise John had given orders that Arthur was to be blinded and castrated, and that Hubert de Burgh, who had charge of him, refused to see it done. But there may have been others less humane and less ready to defy the king. At all events whether Arthur died or whether he lived on as a mutilated captive, he was not seen again; the conflicting rumours of his fate aroused and concerted all King John's enemies.

The war broke out again in the spring of 1203. Swiftly Brittany revolted, and Le Mans capitulated to the French. Later in the year Philip Augustus laid siege to Château Gaillard. Richard's 'Saucy Castle', which he had thought so strategically situated that it would prove impregnable though its walls were built of butter, was confidently defended by its Anglo–Norman Constable, Roger de Lacy. King John planned a skilful relief operation: simultaneously supplies were to be delivered by boats from the Seine, while the besiegers were attacked from the landward side by William Marshal. But the two movements were not successfully synchronized; the relief failed, and after a six months' siege Château Gaillard surrendered on 8 March 1204.

The French advance into the Angevin Empire was swift, and it met with little resistance. Philip Augustus took Falaise, Caen, Bayeux, Cherbourg and Barfleur. The Breton army seized Mont-St-Michel and Avranches. Rouen capitulated on Midsummer Day.

King John had lost Normandy almost unbelievably soon after his victory at Mirebeau. It must have been a bitter realization to him that, with the honourable exception of Roger de Lacy, few of the commanders of his castles or cities had exerted themselves to display loyalty to him. Indeed, they in turn accused him of inertia, and blamed him for infatuated dalliance with his young queen, while his empire crumbled around him.

But the truth was that John had inherited the legacy of a legend: John 'Softsword' was the successor of Richard 'Coeur de Lion'. That the explanation of the success of the one and the failure of the other lay as much in the condition of the exchequer as in the characters of the two kings was beyond the understanding of the facile bestowers of nicknames.

The Quality of Ordinary Life

The lives of ordinary people throughout the Angevin Empire were hard, and the pace of change was slow. The illustrations in this section belong for the most part to the following century, or even to the fourteenth century; but in the course of three hundred years the style of life, governed by the seasons and disrupted only by warfare, would have changed little:

Ploughing with oxen (RADIO TIMES HULTON PICTURE LIBRARY)

Harvesting (BIBLIOTHÈQUE DE DIJON)

Bringing in the harvest (RADIO TIMES HULTON PICTURE LIBRARY)

In England 'franklins' or free tenants might be small farmers of considerable substance; 'villeins' or un-free tenants, who farmed holdings of up to thirty acres, at least enjoyed the advantage of security of tenure; 'cottars' who subsisted by casual labour formed a 'rural proleteriat'

Threshing (BRITISH LIBRARY)

A sheepfold. A woman is shown milking a ewe, and a man tending an ailing sheep. English wool was already a profitable export in the twelfth century, and the Cistercian order of monks, which sheep-farmed extensively, generously donated a year's revenue to the ransom of Richard *Coeur de Lion* (BRITISH LIBRARY)

Killing a pig.
The provision of winter feed for agricultural animals was a problem which the Middle Ages had not solved. Animals were slaughtered in the autumn, and their meat salted to use during the winter (BRITISH LIBRARY)

Bread and meat were considered to be more nourishing than vegetables and fruit. A baker making bread in a brick oven of a type of which numerous examples survive and of which a few are still in use (GUILDHALL MUSEUM)

Two birds and a sucking pig roasting on a spit before a fire. Sparks fly upward as one cook stokes the fire while the other turns the spit. Food of this quality would have been a rare feast outside the Great Hall of a castle (BRITISH MUSEUM)

Hawking, the sport of kings, lords and knights, was carried on with little regard for the agricultural labourer, or the land on which the supply of basic foods depended (MANSELL COLLECTION)

Two women ferreting: sport, food-supply and pest-control agreeably combined (BRITISH LIBRARY)

The entertainments which enlivened the harsh business of everyday life were simple:

A man puts a performing monkey through its paces (BRITISH MUSEUM)

Monks and nuns play a game which has been somewhat speciously identified as an early form of cricket (BODLEIAN LIBRARY, OXFORD)

Simple forms of mechanisation were gradually introduced. A diagrammatic drawing of a watermill; the millrace contains fishtraps, which were condemned in Clause Thirty-Three of Magna Carta (BRITISH LIBRARY)

A walled town. The building of new towns was a feature of the age. Towns had to be defensible because of the prevailing method of siege warfare; therefore new towns were built to meet the needs of economic growth, instead of old towns being permitted to spread beyond their existing defences (TRINITY COLLEGE, CAMBRIDGE)

A leper and a cripple approach a town to beg for alms. While the Christian duty of almsgiving was performed by religious foundations and enjoined by the Church as the duty of the affluent, society left the welfare of the unfortunate to the individual conscience (GIRAUDON)

The possible fate of the malefactor: execution for murder, castration for rape, mutilation of a hand for theft. In reality these crimes were frequently punished by a fine, or punishment was avoided by seeking the privilege of sanctuary (CORPUS CHRISTI COLLEGE, CAMBRIDGE)

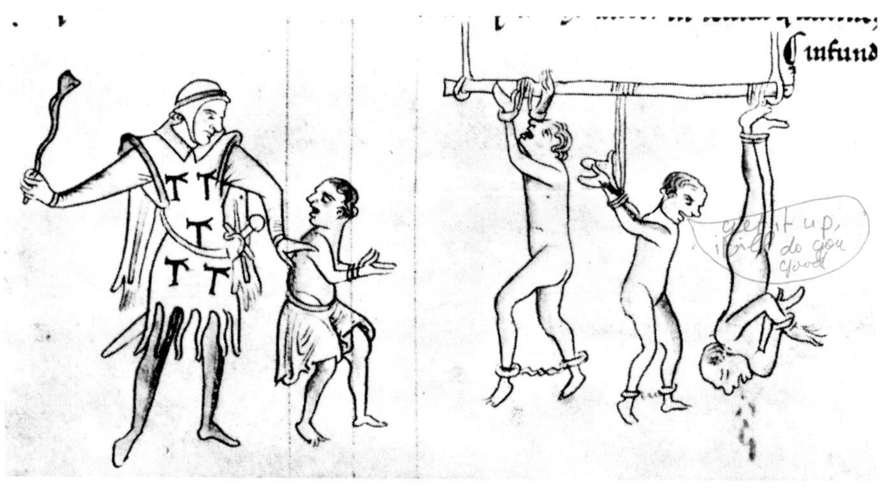

II
Contest with the Pope

John
I am making what I want to make
In the manner I want to make it.
The English are mine
And what I want I shall take it,
Or provide it, when I want,
In the manner of my father . . .

(John Arden, *Left-Handed Liberty*, Act I, Scene I)

For the first time since the Norman Conquest, England was threatened by an alien invader. The King of France was preparing to cross the Channel. The English, and the Anglo–Normans who by now had come to identify themselves with England, prepared to resist the foreigners from the Île de France.

King John organized a 'Commune' – a comprehensive home guard – of which every man or boy over the age of twelve had to become a member. In the spring of 1205 he ordered that groups of nine knights should equip and pay a tenth knight to serve in defence of England overseas; but, in the event of a French invasion, all knights were to be ready to take arms to defend the kingdom.

Losses on the Continent continued to whittle away the Angevin Empire but the expected invasion of England did not take place. In 1206 King John was able to resume the initiative. He landed at La Rochelle, which was still in his possession, and during the summer he recaptured Montauban and Angers. When a two years' truce was negotiated in the autumn it seemed possible that his losses might be redeemed.

While King John's attention was directed to the defence of England, and to foreign wars, Hubert Walter died. At the time of his death he was both chancellor and justiciar, as well as Archbishop of Canterbury. In him England lost a great administrator, not a great primate; but both required to be replaced, and King John naturally wished to see both replaced in one person.

King John thought he had found another Hubert Walter in John de Gray,

Bishop of Norwich. However, in securing the appointment of his candidate John did not have the easiest of popes to deal with. Innocent III was an exceptionally vigorous man, who had been only thirty-seven when he was elected pope. Spirituality and political ambition were integrated in his personality. He was unlikely to accept any king's nominee for any bishopric without stringent enquiry.

Henry II had once directed the monks of Winchester to elect a new bishop, in the following terms: 'I order you to hold a free election, but, nonetheless, I forbid you to elect anyone except Richard my clerk, the Archdeacon of Poitiers.' Having issued his orders and had them obeyed, Henry could expect the relatively insecure Pope Alexander III to accept his choice. But the power of the Papacy had been steadily recovering, and John could not assume that Innocent III would be so complaisant.

The monks of Canterbury wanted to elect as archbishop their own sub-prior Reginald, as in accordance with canonical – though much-abused – principles, they had the right to do. They duly elected him, and sent him to Rome for his consecration. King John, who had hoped to impose his nominee on the monks and then request papal approval of the so-called election, was exceedingly angry that custom and privilege had been flouted. He complained to the pope.

Innocent listened to both sides of the story, and decided to accept neither Reginald nor John de Gray. He summoned fifteen monks from Canterbury to Rome, and subjected them to the pressure of his own influence. The result was the unanimous election of the pope's own candidate, Cardinal Stephen Langton.

It was obvious that in putting forward a nominee of his own the pope was earnestly desirous of achieving a compromise, and the choice he made was a good one. Stephen Langton was an Englishman, whose qualities of wisdom and diplomacy were amply displayed in later years. He had a great reputation for learning and probity. He had lectured at the University of Paris, and had lately become Cardinal of St Chrysogonus. Though he had been long absent from England, he identified himself with the interests of his native land when eventually he became its primate.

Unfortunately King John refused to accept Stephen Langton as Archbishop of Canterbury, for no better reason than that the choice was not his own but the pope's. Innocent would not alter his decision at the bidding of any secular ruler. A genuine attempt at compromise resulted in a confrontation between two obstinate men; their clash of wills was prolonged into a six-year conflict.

On 23 March 1208 the bishops of London, Ely and Worcester, at the command of the pope, laid the sentence of Interdict upon England.

As had happened a few years previously in France, the religious life of the community almost ceased. The people of England in their turn grew accustomed to living surrounded only by the sounds of the countryside, for the church bells, which had ceaselessly pealed and tolled, summoning them to Mass or announcing the Consecration, each with a different and identifiable voice, were silenced. People learned to arrange for the essential sacraments – baptism, marriage and the confession of the dying – to take place in privacy, almost in secrecy. The dead were 'interred in woods or ditches by the road side without prayer or priest'.

Innocent III had consecrated Stephen Langton as Archbishop of Canterbury on 17 July 1207 and, though the Interdict had been threatened the following month, time for negotiation had been allowed before it was imposed, but all negotiations had broken down.

The bishops who pronounced the sentence of Interdict naturally found it necessary to flee the country, and Langton himself was forbidden to set foot in England. A few months previously John had quarrelled with Archbishop Geoffrey Plantagenet about financial matters, and Geoffrey had excommunicated the collectors of a tax to which he objected, and had then left England. So, at the beginning of the Interdict, the sees of Canterbury, York, London, Ely and Worcester were unoccupied. The bishoprics of Lincoln, Chichester and Exeter happened to be vacant, following the deaths of their bishops, and during the next few months the bishops of Durham and Coventry died.

Since the sentence of Interdict did not break down King John's resistance, the pope excommunicated him in November 1209, whereupon the bishops of Bath, Salisbury and Rochester felt obliged to join the surviving English bishops in exile. The only bishops who remained at their posts were John de Gray, who doubtless felt that he owed loyalty to a king who had defied the pope on his behalf, and Peter des Roches, the Poitevin Bishop of Winchester, who, like Hubert Walter, was an administrator first and a churchman second.

The English Church was thus left without leaders, and at the mercy of King John, who retaliated against the Interdict by confiscating the property of the clergy, both monastic and secular. However, King John's retaliation was worse in the report than in the reality, for he allowed abbeys and monasteries to continue farming, and to retain enough produce to provide 'reasonable maintenance', and he likewise allotted a subsistence allowance to secular clergy.

But he indulged himself in a characteristic jest at the expense of the parish clergy by taking into custody all the women who were euphemistically described as priests' 'housekeepers', but who were frequently their mistresses. The clergy were obliged to reveal their reliance on the services of their womenfolk by ransoming them from the king.

After King John had been excommunicated, his measures against the Church grew correspondingly more punitive. The gain to the exchequer from sequestrated monastic property has been estimated at over 100,000 marks. Some of the monastic communities which were particularly hard hit dispersed, and individual monks took refuge in other houses of their order.

Stephen Langton spent his years of exile at the Cistercian Abbey of Pontigny, which had once harboured Becket. Possibly his place of refuge was chosen for reasons of symbolism: he was prepared to play Becket's part to the end, if the need arose.

During the years of the Interdict, King John, far from allowing his political activity to be circumscribed by his quarrel with the pope, displayed the formidable energy which he had inherited from his father, in diverse enterprises.

His long-term ambition was to regain his lost continental lands, but he was far-sighted enough to consider that he would be in a stronger position for doing so if he could risk turning his back on his neighbours. Richard I had given no personal attention to relations with Scotland, Ireland and Wales, and in consequence he had left John another legacy of trouble.

William the Lion, King of Scots, had, it may be remembered, purchased his full independence from Richard, and had refused to back John in making trouble while Richard was imprisoned. However, the kings of Scots had once possessed the counties of Cumberland, Westmorland and Northumberland, and William aspired to recover them. By 1209 he was growing old, and John was weary of parrying his claims with words and border skirmishes. He led an army as far as Norham where he parleyed with the old Scots king, who decided on a treaty in preference to a pitched battle.

King William withdrew his claim to the three counties, and handed over his two daughters as hostages. Three years later he sent his son Alexander to John's court, and after John's death the Scottish prince, who had become King Alexander II, married John's eldest daughter Joan. Thereafter, for a time, Anglo–Scottish relations were more neighbourly than warlike.

Ireland received a visit from King John in 1210. He had been there before, in 1185, after his father had turned a deaf ear to his pleas to be allowed to accept the throne of Jerusalem. Created 'Lord of Ireland', John had been despatched to make his fortune and to extend the Angevin domains. No doubt he would have become King of Ireland had his expedition been successful, but he had been too immature for such an enterprise. He was reported to have pulled the beards of Irish chieftains, spent the war chest provided for him on riotous living, and ignored the advice of the Anglo–Norman barons already established in Ireland. John's return to his father had been swift and ignominious.

In 1210 it was the Anglo–Norman barons who represented John's chief problem. John was still titular Lord of Ireland, but his justiciar in Ireland, Meiler FitzHenry, was by no means as powerful as some of his compatriots. William Marshal, for instance, besides being Earl of Pembroke, was Lord of Leinster in Ireland; William de Briouze, as well as holding great estates in

Wales, was Lord of Limerick. In fact, John had quarrelled with both of them before he undertook his second expedition to Ireland.

John's failure to get on with his barons, as a result of his inability to give or to inspire trust, has been remarked upon already. As he grew older his innate suspiciousness, which poisoned his relations with many of his powerful subjects, gained an increasing hold on him. His numerous sly tricks for keeping himself informed of everyone's doings grew so intricate that occasionally he lost track of what he was doing. Once he wrote to his chamberlain, reminding him that he had given orders that nobody must communicate with a particular prisoner except in the presence of three members of the royal household 'and because we do not well recollect who those three were, inform us thereupon, that another time we may with more certainty give you our commands.'

King John was unnecessarily suspicious of William Marshal's loyalty, because William – in perfect accord with his feudal obligations – had done homage to Philip Augustus for some lands which he held in France. John summoned William Marshal to come to court in 1207, and encouraged Meiler FitzHenry to harry his Irish lands in his absence. William's knights decisively defeated the Justiciar of Ireland, so John decided to make his peace. William was confirmed as Lord of Leinster, and permitted to return to it, leaving two of his sons with the king as hostages.

Even this treatment did not shake William Marshal's loyalty to King John, but he did not hesitate to anger him afresh in 1210, when he attempted to shield William de Briouze from the king's wrath.

Exactly what Briouze had done to offend the king is not known, but in 1207 John had seized all his castles and estates in Wales and had demanded two of his sons as hostages. It was told, admittedly by one of the less reliable chroniclers, that Briouze's wife Matilda said to her husband:

'I will not deliver my sons to your Lord, King John, for he foully murdered his nephew Arthur, whom he should have cared for honourably.'

Perhaps William de Briouze did indeed know the truth about Arthur's fate, which he had told his wife, and perhaps she made the fateful error of speaking publicly of it. At all events, Matilda de Briouze was the single exception to John's customarily kindly treatment of women: she and one of her sons were captured and imprisoned by John and were never seen again. It was widely rumoured that they were starved to death.

The power of the Briouze family was completely overthrown in Ireland, and during 1210 King John also deposed the Lacy family from the lordship of Meath, and captured from Hugh de Lacy the port and Castle of Carrickfergus. In remarkable contrast with his earlier fiasco in Ireland, on his second expedition there John beat the Anglo-Norman barons into obedience, received the submission of the native Irish princes, and left John de Gray to rule Ireland as an efficient justiciar. William Marshal was still probably the most powerful man in Ireland, but he had no intention of using his power to disturb the king's peace.

During the summer of 1211 John fought a campaign in Wales, where he had a resolute adversary in Llewelyn the Great, Prince of Gwynedd. In 1204 Llewelyn had married John's illegitimate daughter, who like her legitimate half-sister was called Joan. While Llewelyn had remained the ally of his father-in-law, he had begun to extend his power within Wales itself. John did not relish the thought of the Prince of Gwynedd becoming Prince of Wales: he preferred to see Wales weak and divided rather than strong and united.

His aggression almost achieved the opposite of his intentions, for the Welsh concerted to support Llewelyn in his resistance to John's invasion. John's campaign of 1211 was sufficiently successful for Llewelyn to conclude a peace which he regarded as humiliating; but the next year the Welsh took the initiative and captured two castles which were occupied by the English. They took courage from the fact that Welsh aspirations to independence from England were encouraged by Pope Innocent III.

King John mustered his army at Nottingham, and then, quite suddenly, he abandoned the projected campaign, apparently upon receiving intelligence of a plot by some of his English barons to depose and murder him. There may have been such a conspiracy, for after the abandonment of the Welsh campaign two powerful English barons, Eustace de Vesci and Robert Fitz-Walter, fled the country. They had nothing to flee from but the king's suspicions.

Even rumours of a conspiracy give the measure of John's growing unpopularity with the barons of England. They had more to complain of than the king's everlasting suspicion and his unpredictable ways of acting upon it. To lead armies to Scotland, Ireland and Wales cost a great deal of money, which had to be found by John's vassals. His ways of raising money were ingenious, efficient, legal and unpopular.

Though John earned the reputation of a bad king, he did not earn it through being a bad ruler. Indeed, his attention to the daily routine of government was exhaustively thorough; he was far too able and too heavy handed to be well liked by men who would have welcomed opportunities for more freedom of action.

John brought his father's virtues to the task of ruling, and they were virtues which had made Henry II unpopular in his lifetime. John's personal failings raised his unpopularity to a dangerous level.

In 1212 William Marshal gave King John a piece of excellent advice: to make up his quarrel with the pope. Innocent's encouragement of John's Welsh adversaries provided one good reason for doing so. A stronger one was that in the summer of 1211 the papal legate Pandulph had absolved John's subjects from their oath of allegiance to him, and the pope had threatened him with deposition. At the end of 1212 Innocent invited Philip Augustus to assist in implementing the Letters of Deposition which he had despatched to Stephen Langton. With alacrity, Philip prepared to co-operate.

John outmanoeuvred him. No sooner had the pope written to Langton than he received emissaries from King John, who offered to make peace on the pope's terms. These were that John should accept Stephen Langton as Archbishop of Canterbury, that he should allow the return of the exiled English clergy and that he should compensate the Church for the property which he had sequestrated.

King John readily agreed to these terms, and with his characteristic capacity for being too clever by half, he appeared to abase himself at the pope's feet. When the papal legate Pandulph arrived in England, John offered to acknowledge himself a vassal of the pope, to hold England as a fief of the Papal See, and to be 'faithful to God, to St Peter, to the Church of Rome, and to my Liege Lord Pope Innocent and his Catholic successors'. He surrendered his crown to Pandulph, who ceremoniously replaced it.

Stephen Langton arrived in England in the summer of 1213. He received a warm welcome, and released King John from his excommunication. The following summer, after the financial arrangements concerning King John's compensation of the Church had been completed, England was released from the Interdict. Bells rang, churches were opened, weddings were celebrated and funerals solemnized with accustomed pomp.

In the meantime Pope Innocent had commanded Philip Augustus to desist from his plan of invading the kingdom of John, the most favoured and obedient vassal of the Holy See. The subtle-minded King of England had secured his own position, and staved off another projected invasion by his apparent humiliation. Thenceforward he would enjoy a particularly solicitous display of papal favour.

'Thus,' one of John's recent biographers has observed, 'did King John and Pope Innocent III stand on their heads . . . '

III
The King at Bay

God defend
But that I should prove
An easy man to love
But if hatred is their preference
My own posture at this conference
Will be that of a very hedgehog!

(John Arden, *Left-Handed Liberty*, Act II, Scene I)

'Since I became reconciled to God and submitted myself and my kingdom to the Church, nothing has gone well with me.' This remark, attributed to King John in 1214, if truly reported, must have appeared to his hearers to have been justified.

While John was campaigning to exert his authority over his neighbours, his foreign policy was directed to the construction of an effective alliance against Philip Augustus. His efforts proved to have been worthwhile, because Philip did not relinquish his aggressive intentions against England at the command of Innocent III. He was prevented from undertaking his war as a crusade against an excommunicated king, but he did not shrink from naked aggression; he merely altered his tactics, and occupied Flanders as a preliminary to using the Flemish coast as a base for his invasion of England. At least John had gained time to complete his diplomatic preparations.

John's allies formed a powerful coalition which included the counts of Holland and Boulogne, and the emperor's brother the Count Palatine of the Rhine. Otto IV himself was also John's ally, but he was not a strong one, because ever since Richard I had helped to secure his election he had had a hard struggle to maintain his position. In 1210 Innocent III had recognized the rival claimant to the imperial throne, Frederick of Hohenstaufen, as emperor. Frederick was allied with Philip Augustus. Innocent, therefore, had allies on both sides; perhaps he felt that as pope he should take an Olympian view of the conflict.

The Count of Flanders appealed to King John for assistance against the invading French, and in response, John sent a fleet of English ships, loaded with knights and mercenaries, and commanded by William Longsword, Earl of Salisbury, who was a bastard son of Henry II, and a trusted supporter of his half-brother the king. The English shipmasters had plenty of experience of piracy against the French, and the five hundred ships which sailed for Flanders made up a formidable armada.

The Earl of Salisbury found the French fleet in the harbour of Damme, which was the port of Bruges. On 30 May 1213 Philip's ships were for the most part destroyed, and their supplies taken on board by the English. The fact that the English knights landed, and then hastily re-embarked when Philip's army appeared in a belated dash to save his ships, somewhat detracted from the heroic glamour of the action, but its efficacy remained indisputable. Salisbury sailed home in triumph.

King John decided that the time was ripe for him to cross the Channel. A truce with the Welsh provided a temporary solution to the previous year's problems, but the rumours of conspiracy which had led him to call off his second Welsh campaign left him with grave doubts of the loyalty of his English barons.

Under the terms of his reconciliation with the pope, John had been obliged to allow the return to England of Eustace de Vesci and Robert FitzWalter, together with the exiled clergy. De Vesci was Lord of Alnwick in Northumberland, and the possessor of great influence in the North of England. After his return from exile his disloyalty was frankly revealed when he led a group principally composed of northern barons into open defiance of the king. 'With one mind and determination', as a well-informed chronicler put it, they refused to accompany King John on any campaign outside his kingdom, and they refused the usual alternative of paying 'scutage' ('shield tax') to purchase exemption from military service.

A considerable proportion of John's unpopularity arose from his demanding scutage with increasing frequency. Lord and knights without estates abroad especially disliked being required to leave England, and resented being obliged to pay scutage if they did not go. Whichever they resented more, John preferred to levy scutage, because the proceeds paid the wages of mercenaries, who were more obedient and better trained in warfare than most of his vassals. Frequent scutage at ever-increasing rates gave John's vassals a valid reason for complaint, but the legal question of who was or was not obliged to fight for the king on the other side of the Channel was far from clear.

In the late summer of 1213 John was in favour of using his mercenaries to discipline de Vesci and his supporters by force of arms; but Stephen Langton, exercising his powers of diplomacy for the first time, managed to dissuade him, and arranged a temporary reconcilliation between the king and the disaffected northerners.

During the autumn of 1213 the first mention was made of the desirability of a definitive settlement of regal and baronial rights, as a means of preventing inconclusive confrontations in the future. Stephen Langton is said to have reminded the northerners that Henry I had issued a coronation charter which defined his powers; but in all probability they did not need reminding. Raking up evidence of the superior customs of the past was the usual method of highlighting the abuses of the present. Many of the highly taxed and heavily disciplined vassals of King John were ready to believe that before the Plantagenets had ruled, England had enjoyed a desirable condition of freedom. Men who had lived in the reigns of William the Conqueror and William Rufus would have disagreed; and whatever limitations of power Henry I had conceded in his coronation charter, he had ruled with a heavy hand. But the influence which the falsification of history can have upon politics is very great. In this instance it eventually led to King John's setting his seal to one of the most famous of all documents.

King John sailed from Portsmouth on 2 February 1214, leaving Peter des Roches, Bishop of Winchester, as justiciar, with Stephen Langton and the papal legate Nicholas, Bishop of Tusculum, to assist him. John's mistrust of his lay magnates is clearly illustrated by his leaving England under exclusively ecclesiastical control, though his vassalage to the pope may also have suggested that this structure of action would be appropriate.

The king's fleet reached La Rochelle on 15 February. His intention was to subject Philip Augustus to the double pressure of invasion from Poitou and from Flanders, where John's allies were likewise preparing to make war.

John occupied the spring and early summer in complicated military manoeuvres in Poitou, Anjou and the county of La Marche, to the north of Limoges. The intricacy of his movements was directed partly by the exigencies of local events, partly by his desire to keep Philip Augustus guessing what he would do next.

His campaign was not devoid of successes. He received the homage of many Poitevin barons, including the powerful and troublesome Lusignans, after he had besieged and taken two of their strongholds. In mid-June he captured Nantes and recaptured Angers – but that was the last of his victories. He was besieging the newly-built fortress of La Roche-au-Moine, near Angers, when Philip's son, the Dauphin Louis, marched to its relief. Many of John's Poitevin barons, who probably held lands from Philip as well as John, refused to take arms against Philip's son. John was obliged to raise the siege, and at the beginning of July he returned to La Rochelle.

In the meantime Philip, leaving Louis to contain King John's forces, turned his attention to events in Flanders. On 27 July 1214, at the decisive battle of Bouvines, he defeated a huge army which included the combined forces of the Emperor Otto and the counts of Holland, Flanders and Boulogne, and a detachment of King John's mercenaries commanded by the Earl of Salisbury.

William Longsword of Salisbury was captured by the Bishop of Beauvais, who knocked him senseless with a club; the bishop, like many other churchmen, was prepared to enter a battle, but not to wield a sword. The counts of Boulogne and Flanders were also taken prisoner. The emperor fled when he saw that defeat was inevitable, but since he had risked his life sufficiently to have had three horses killed under him, no one thought that his escape was cowardly.

King John's limited successes might have led on to victory had his allies won the battle of Bouvines, but the disaster in Flanders left him in too weak a position to prolong the war. At the end of August a preliminary truce was made, which on 18 September was extended into a truce for five years. King John and King Philip agreed that each should keep the territories which he held at that date, and King John secured the release of Salisbury by exchanging him for a kinsman of Philip's who had been captured at Nantes.

The question of the rival emperor was settled in 1218 by the death of Otto IV and the succession of Frederick of Hohenstaufen as Frederick II. He was one of the most remarkable personalities of the Middle Ages, whose brilliant intellect and varied talents earned him the nickname of '*Stupor Mundi*' ('The Wonder of the World').

In the meantime King John, in the autumn of 1214, returned to England, to face the reckoning compounded of military failure and baronial resentment.

It was by an unjust stroke of fate that King John never recovered from the consequences of the battle of Bouvines, which he personally had not lost. When John landed in England once more, on 15 October 1214, it was with the reputation of a defeated general, which was of little advantage to him in dealing with the recalcitrant subjects he had left behind when he departed on his campaign.

During his absence Peter des Roches had kept order in England, but his stern discipline had made him increasingly unpopular, and by extension his own unpopularity had enhanced that of King John. By the time that John returned, the number of malcontents had grown, and the causes of resentment had proliferated. The scutage which John levied to fight campaigns abroad was unpopular; the mercenaries whose pay the tax provided, some of whom returned to England with the king, were unpopular. The king's reliance upon ecclesiastical counsellors was unpopular, especially among those lay magnates who felt that their influence, reckoned in the terms of the size of the estates which they held and the number of knights they had 'enfeoffed', entitled them to be the official advisers and ministers of the king. New forms of taxation, such as customs duties, which affected the pockets of barons who had entered the world of commerce, as well as those of merchants, merely served to add new insults to existing injuries.

At the hot centre of the volcano which was about to erupt was the group of northerners who had defied the king and refused him either service or scutage. The king had not withdrawn his demands for the tax, and the attempts by exchequer officials to collect it during the autumn of 1214 raised baronial tempers to white heat.

Besides Eustace de Vesci, other northerners who were approaching the point of rebellion against the king were Robert de Ros and Roger de Montbegon, Robert Grelley, Lord of Manchester, and Gilbert de Gant, who besides holding estates in the north was a claimant to the earldom of Lincoln. But the opposition to King John was not exclusively northern: Robert FitzWalter was the Lord of Dunmow in Essex, and Geoffrey de Mandeville, Earl of Essex, and Roger Bigod, Earl of Norfolk, were equally active in resisting what they regarded as King John's arbitrary rule.

That rule, however, had shown sufficient merits to have held for King John the loyalty of a number of vassals who were personally too powerful to be suspected of time-serving. William Marshal's loyalty to each of the the Plantagenet kings in turn had proved unshakeable; and John found two powerful supporters even in the disaffected north, Ranulf, Earl of Chester, and William de Ferrers, Earl of Derby. He could also count on the support of the clerics who had been the caretakers of England in his absence.

John turned to the Church, as the division of his vassals into the categories of supporters and opponents gave advance warning of a major rebellion. He wrote to Innocent III, informing him of events in England. Possibly both to increase his credit with the pope, and to attempt to create a diversion from events in England, he took the Cross.

The previous year the pope had attempted to reconcile John and Philip Augustus sufficiently to persuade them to undertake a new Crusade together. He was delighted to hear of John's vow, and in the hope of hastening the crusade he wrote to John urging him to hear the complaints of his subjects favourably. Since King John's opponents had also written to the pope stating their case, they received a letter from Innocent commanding them not to conspire or rebel against their king. Stephen Langton was soundly reproved for not having mediated successfully between them.

Innocent III was too far from the centre of action to be informed accurately of what was happening in England, and his reproof of Langton was less than just, for it was as a mediator that Langton laboured from first to last. In his efforts to prevent the outbreak of civil war Langton was assisted by William Marshal, whom the king appointed as his deputy to treat with the rebellious barons, since John himself refused to meet them.

When King John heard from Langton and William Marshal the concessions which his recalcitrant subjects required him to make, and the promises with which they wished him to set limits to his future powers, his answer was short and to the point:

'Why not ask for my kingdom?'

Upon the undoubtedly predicted report that King John had refused their terms, the already committed rebels renounced their homage to him, and appointed Robert FitzWalter the commander of their army. They called it 'The Army of God and the Holy Church', which probably illustrated exactly what they thought of King John's relationship with the pope, and of the sincerity of his Crusader's vow. However, most men throughout history have wanted to think that they fought with God on their side.

The war was very brief. It began on 12 May 1215, when King John ordered the confiscation of the estates of the rebels, and officially it ended on 15 June. In the meantime the advantage of war went to the rebels when London was betrayed to them by a minority of the citizens. The majority had supported King John since he had recently granted London an advantageous charter of civic liberties. Many borough charters which date from the reign of King John were granted for the motive of gaining, simultaneously, revenue and support. London, however, fell to the rebels, and the fall of the city occasioned renewed persecution of the Jews. Many of the rebels had been obliged to borrow from the Jews in order to meet King John's tax demands, and in the capture of the city they saw the way to recoup themselves. Once they had occupied the city, they laid siege to the Tower of London.

King John accepted the need to treat for peace, and once again it was Stephen Langton and William Marshal who played the leading parts in negotiating the settlement. When an acceptable set of peace terms had been hammered out the king came from his headquarters at Windsor and the rebels came from London to meet on the bank of the Thames, at the famous spot which on the peace treaty itself was named 'the meadow that is called Runnymede between Windsor and Staines'.

The document to which King John set his seal on 15 June 1215 was a peace treaty made between the opposing forces in a civil war. It was not an attempt by a particular social class to impose its will on a king, and in so doing to change the character of England. Certainly it was not an attempt to define principles of government for England which should be applicable for all time. It was not an expression of the unanimous opinion of the barons of England; it was not even an expression of the unanimous views of King John's opponents. It was probably an expression of the best that the mediators could achieve for both sides after they had reasoned with both King John and his opponents.

The peace treaty was cast in the form of sixty-three promises made by the king to his subjects. Some of them referred to relatively minor grievances:

'Henceforth all fishtraps shall be cleared completely from the Thames and the Medway and throughout all England, except along the sea coast.' (Clause 33)

Some of them referred to matters of immediate concern:

'As soon as peace is restored we will remove from the kingdom all foreign knights, crossbowmen, serjeants and mercenaries, who have come with horses and arms to the detriment of the kingdom.' (Clause 51)

Some state principles which no longer affect living issues:

'No one shall be arrested upon the appeal [accusation] of a woman for the death of anyone except her husband.' (Clause 54)

In fact, much of it would make disappointing reading for anyone who expected it to resemble the American Declaration of Independence. Yet, though the peace treaty sealed at Runnymede was a document framed to fulfil the demands of a specific set of circumstances, some of its clauses contain statements of principle which remain applicable in any century because of their obvious good sense:

'We will not make justices, constables, sheriffs and bailiffs save of such as know the law of the kingdom and mean to observe it well.' (Clause 45)

Two clauses have stood out from the rest, resonant, grandiloquent, and often quoted:

'No freeman shall be arrested or imprisoned or disseised [deprived of his land] or outlawed or exiled or in any way destroyed, neither will we set forth against him, except by the lawful judgment of his peers [equals] and by the law of the land.' (Clause 39)

'To no one will we sell, to no one will we refuse or delay right or justice.' (Clause 40)

A committee of twenty-five barons was appointed to see that the promises made in the sixty-three clauses were duly observed, and copies of it were distributed to every shire of the kingdom. The document was felt to be important at the time because it had been framed to re-establish peace in England, and to provide guidelines to the way in which peace could be maintained.

It seemed a sufficiently good expression of the laws and customs of England for the regency of John's son to re-issue it in the year of his accession, 1216. The following year it was re-issued in a slightly different form: the clauses referring to forest law were issued in a separate document or charter. Again in 1225 two charters were issued, and referred to as the large charter ('Magna Carta') and the small one.

So it was that years after King John's death the charter based on the peace treaty of Runnymede became 'Magna Carta'. Its greater fame developed centuries later. In the early seventeenth century, a period of constitutional upheaval when the growing power of the House of Commons was beginning to be asserted against the rule of the House of Stuart, Magna Carta was almost rediscovered, and became venerated by those who sought to extend the power of Parliament, as the greatest expression of the liberties of the subject.

The debt which the English owed to Magna Carta became an unquestioned tenet of popular belief. As Kipling expressed it:

> And still when mob or monarch lays
> Too rude a hand on English ways
> The whisper wakes, the shudder plays,
>   Across the reeds at Runnymede.
>   And Thames, that knows the moods of Kings,
>   And crowds and priests and suchlike things,
>   Rolls deep and dreadful as his brings
>   Their warning down from Runnymede!

The popular legend dies hard that the barons of England forced King John to sign Magna Carta; but had the king been opposed by the unanimous will of his vassals there would have been no need for rebellion, no opposing forces to join in a civil war, and certainly no necessity for an elaborate peace treaty to end it.

In 1215 King John merely felt that he had been manoeuvred into an awkward situation and made to sign a peace treaty which placed him at a disadvantage. As a first step to righting the situation he requested Pope Innocent III to absolve him from the obligation to abide by the terms of the treaty. Pope Innocent, who took the same view, obliged him on 12 August 1215.

The Knight's World

A twelfth-century knight wearing a chainmail, surcoat and helmet, and armed with a sword. His shield is decorated with the armorial bearings which enabled friends and foes to identify him. The study of armorial bearings eventually developed into the complex science of heraldry. The knight was principally a mounted soldier, and he aspired to become a landholder by being granted a fief by a powerful lord. The most strongly stressed of knightly virtues was that of loyalty to the lord. At best a knight might be a chivalrous Christian hero like William Marshal, at worst he might be an unscrupulous ruffian (VICTORIA & ALBERT MUSEUM)

A carving of a knight slaying a dragon: probably an allegorical representation of the struggle between good and evil, showing the good knight overcoming the power of the adversary of mankind (J. C. D. SMITH)

Ladies are taken prisoner and fettered: a representation of unchivalrous reality (CORPUS CHRISTI COLLEGE, CAMBRIDGE)

The solemn ritual of the bestowing of knighthood was intended to instil into the recipient a serious intention to practise knightly virtues.

A knight receives his sword from a king (THE DEAN AND CHAPTER OF DURHAM CATHEDRAL)

Young knights are girded with their swords (PICTUREPOINT)

The loyalty of a knight to his lord or suzerain was expressed by the oath of homage. A knight kneels to offer homage to his lord (PETER CLAYTON)

A knight's career demanded a high standard of military proficiency, which had to be maintained by constant practice. A knight practises at a quintain. The knight strikes the shield with his lance and the weighted sack at the other end of the crossbeam swings round, to unhorse him unless he rides swiftly out of the way (BRITISH MUSEUM)

A tournament, or mock battle, in which knights kept in practice for real warfare. Tournaments offered opportunities to win rich prizes, for if a knight was captured in a tournament, just as in war, he had to ransom himself; if his horse was captured it became the victor's property (MANSELL COLLECTION)

A knight's end: death and burial, the common lot of humanity. This magnificently vigorous effigy of an unknown knight suggests not repose in death, but eternal readiness to 'fight the good fight' (PICTUREPOINT)

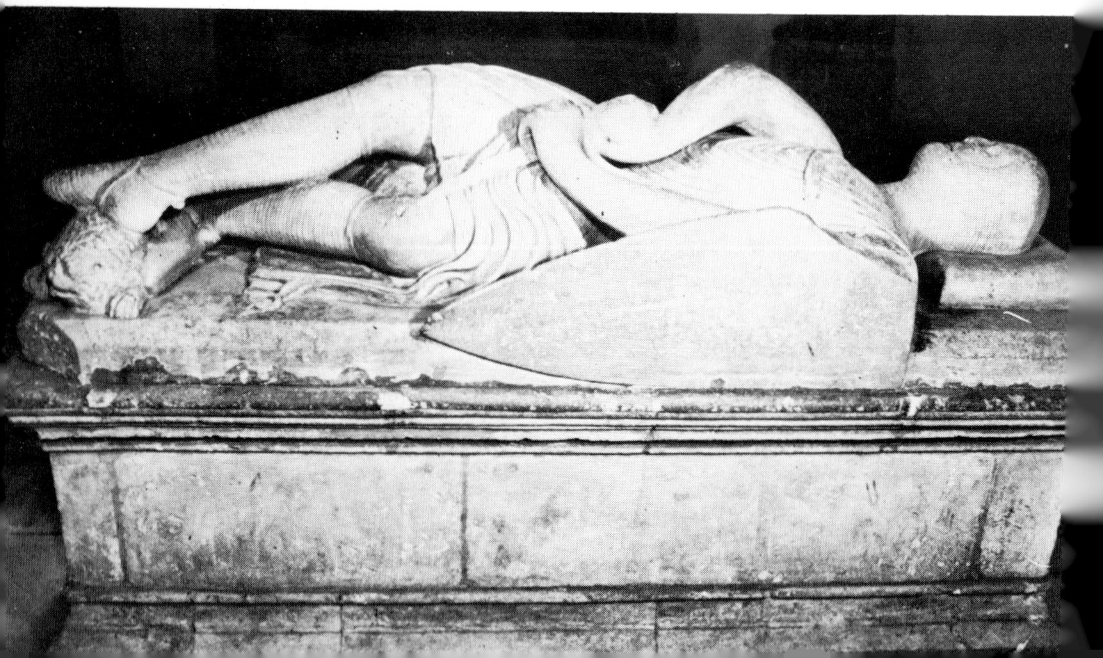

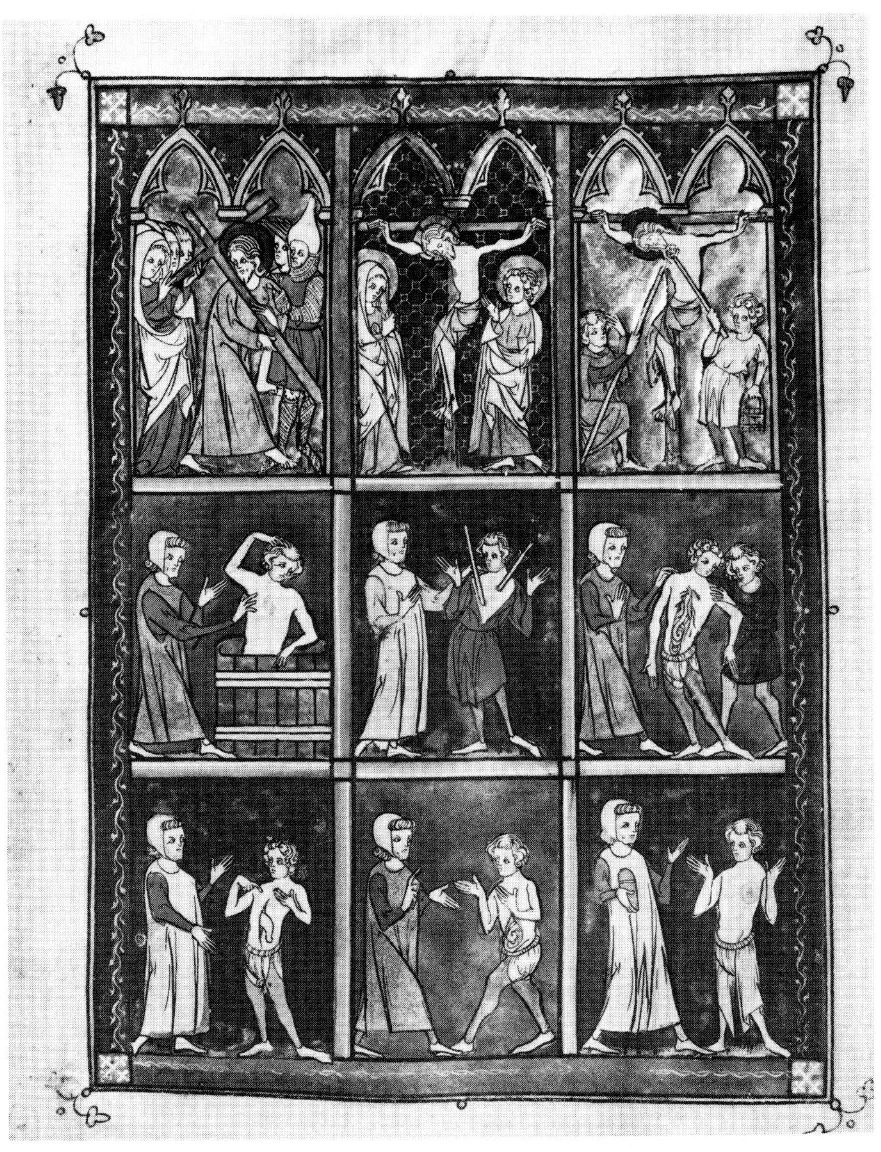

Scene illustrating treatment of wounds from the Chirurgia *of Roger de Salerno. Doctors trained at the famous medical school of Salerno enjoyed great renown, but their skills were unavailing against infection. More knights died as a result of infected wounds than as a direct consequence of injuries in battle* (BRITISH LIBRARY)

The castle was the essential setting of the knight's world. A knight might be appointed constable or 'castellan' of a castle belonging to his lord; a less important knight would be required to perform the duty of 'castle guard' for a specified time each year. A reconstruction drawing of Framlingham Castle, Norfolk, as it would have appeared in the twelfth century (DEPARTMENT OF THE ENVIRONMENT, CROWN COPYRIGHT)

The end of the knight's world: the ruins of Framlingham Castle as they appear today (A. F. KERSTING). *In the words of the troubadour Bertram de Born:*

Kingdoms there are, but no more kings,
And counties, but no counts dwell there,
No marcher from the marches springs,
Castles, domains, lie void and bare;
Gone are the mighty castellans . . .

IV
The Last of the Crowned Lions

'A great Prince certainly, thought scarcely a happy one.'
(The Barnwell Annalist, of King John)

On 12 October 1215 King John stood on the bank of the river Wellstream, which flowed into the Wash on the borders of Lincolnshire and Norfolk. The Wellstream estuary was four and a half miles wide, almost dry at low tide, but treacherous with quicksands. There was a path across it, which the wise traveller walked accompanied by a guide who tested the firmness of the sand with a pole.

King John, on his way from King's Lynn to Lincoln, had crossed the river and halted to watch the long train of baggage wagons negotiating the dangerous route. It was a misty autumn evening, and the tide was beginning to come in. The horses floundered and the heavy carts began to sink as the waters covered the sand. Whether the baggage train had strayed from the route, or whether the wagons were too heavily loaded for the shifting ground to support, cannot be known; but in the words of a chronicler, 'the ground opened in the midst of the waters, and whirlpools sucked in everything, men and horses.'

Some of the wagons were loaded with King John's treasure, composed, according to his most eminent biographer, of 'the jewels he had collected with a connoisseur's delight from far and wide, dozens of gold and silver goblets, flagons, basins, candelabra, phylacteries, pendants and ornaments, the coronation regalia, plus the regalia which his grandmother (Matilda) had worn as Empress of Germany – the great crown, the golden wand with a dove, the sword of Tristram – all were sucked down into the quicksands of the Wellstream.'

King John rode into the water in frantic despair, and was forced back by the danger to his person. From the bank he watched, helpless and hopeless, as all the treasure of his reign was engulfed, just as the quicksands of fortune seemed to be engulfing all that remained of his aspirations and achievements.

Pope Innocent III's annulment of the treaty made at Runnymede had been a signal for the resumption of civil war. Stephen Langton, far from being given any credit for his efforts to make peace, was suspended from his episcopal duties for refusing to excommunicate King John's enemies. In his bitterness of spirit he contemplated resigning his archbishopric and becoming a monk, or even a hermit.

The civil war had gone against King John at the beginning, and Philip Augustus, seeing his chance to destroy the last of the Plantagenet lions, had allowed his son Louis to invade England. Philip had no wish to incur further spiritual penalties from Innocent III, but Louis had a line of attack which might avoid them. His argument was that John was not the rightful King of England because he had been condemned for treason during the reign of Richard I (which ignored the fact that Richard had forgiven him), and that he had murdered the lawful heir, Arthur of Brittany. Louis therefore claimed the English throne in right of his wife, Blanche of Castile, the granddaughter of Henry II.

John fought back, displaying the lion-like courage of his race, though Louis occupied London, and received the support of the king's opponents of the previous year. Young King Alexander II of Scotland attempted a diversion to assist the rebels, and for a time William Longsword of Salisbury threw in his lot with them. But in the renewed civil war King John did not lack loyal supporters. The strong castle of Dover, which Henry II had rebuilt, was defended for him by Hubert de Burgh. The septuagenarian William Marshal remained as loyal as ever, and so did the Earl of Chester. It was a stroke of good fortune for John that Eustace de Vesci and Geoffrey de Mandeville were both killed. William Longsword thought better of his defection and renewed his allegiance to his half-brother.

As autumn came on King John was waging war resolutely. He had stamped out the sparks of rebellion in Cambridgeshire and entered East Anglia, where, on 11 October, he was welcomed and feasted at King's Lynn.

Like his great-grandfather Henry I, he did not stop to consider the effects of heavy feasting on a hard-used body which was not as healthy as it had once been. He forgot his difficulties and anxieties in the pleasures of the table, which included plenty of good peaches washed down with many draughts of fresh cider.

The next day he was suffering from dysentery. Yet he was determined to push on to relieve Lincoln, where a lady was defending the castle against the rebels. Dame Nicola de la Hay was hereditary constable of Lincoln, and she was holding it loyally. The situation had urgency in it, and King John, ill as he was, forced his army of Savary de Mauléon's mercenaries on its way – the route which crossed the Wellstream estuary. He was ill and weary when he saw treasure, men and horses sucked down into the hungry sand.

He lay that night at the Cistercian abbey of Swineshead, and the next day, still weaker, he struggled on to Sleaford. His last day's journey was to the castle of the Bishop of Lincoln at Newark. There King John took to his bed, and the Abbot of Croxton who had great medical skill was brought to attend him. But he was beyond the help of medicine, so the abbot acted as his confessor and performed the last rites for him. On the night of 18 October 1216 King John died, leaving his kingdom torn by civil war, but his cause by no means lost.

It was redeemed by his loyal followers who crowned his son Henry, 'a pretty little knight' of nine years old. In the abbey church of Gloucester a gold circlet belonging to his mother Queen Isabelle was placed on his head by the Bishop of Winchester. Old William Marshal became his regent. Though the crown of England had sunk in the quicksands, a new crown would be made to symbolize a new age.

During the next few months rebels and invaders were defeated, or sought terms with the new regime. On 12 September 1217 peace was made, and the new reign had its true beginning.

By that time it was almost a year since King John had died. In accordance with his last command his body had been carried across England from Newark to Worcester, to be buried in the cathedral, in front of the altar of St Wulfstan, who was his patron. At the end of a life in which he had manipulated religious institutions to serve his own purposes, he may have felt the need of a patron saint.

England had seen the last of King John, who has always had the reputation of a bad man and a bad king; but a contemporary who did not waste words on vulgar vituperation soberly described him as 'a great prince certainly, though scarcely a happy one'.

King John's subjects had seen the last of him in life, but not in death, for his tomb was opened in 1797, and a witness of the event wrote the following description:

> The venerable shrine of this Monarch was opened on Monday last in consequence of a general reparation of the Cathedral Church at Worcester. The remains of the illustrious personage appears entire, his robes, in which he was interred, they are undecayed, though the colour through length of time is indiscernible; on one side of him lay a sword, the bones of his left arm lying on his breast, his teeth, quite perfect, his feet stood erect . . . his remains measured five feet five inches being his stature when living.

It was fitting that he should have been buried with a sword beside him, for like his father and brother he fought indomitably in the defence of his kingship; and with his kingship, in his own convictions, his kingdom was equated.

Index